PRAISE FOR
SAVING OUR SONS

"It is always heartening to see women step up to the writer's table. When the results are as adroit and affecting as Marita Golden's work, it is more than satisfying; it is a cause for celebration."

—**Toni Morrison**, Nobel Laureate

"Marita Golden has captured the special pain that shadows the joy of Black parenthood in these turbulent times. Elegantly written, this book is a breakthrough."

—*Chicago Tribune*

"A wonderful storyteller, an uncompromising mind, Marita Golden explores the African-American experience in a completely original way."

—*Newsweek*

"In this book, Marita reminds us why every black parent should be vigilant and intentional in considering how to steer young black boys—and girls as well—through the precarious passage to adulthood. *Saving Our Sons* is disturbingly relevant in this, the twenty-first century. It's a compelling read."

—**Nathan McCall**, author of *Makes Me Wanna Holler: A Young Black Man in America*

"Marita Golden's *Saving Our Sons* was revelatory when first published and remains so today. *Saving Our Sons* is a superb mother's, artist's, teacher's, and community activist's love story of her son and by extension, all Black sons. This is a book that provides life lessons for our daughters too. *Saving Our Sons* is critical as a guide, motivator, love-note, and an avenue into lifesaving discussions of the heart for all Black children."

—**Haki R. Madhubuti,** founder of Third World Press and author of *Black Men: Obsolete, Single, Dangerous* (1991) and *Taught By Women: Poems As Resistance Language, New and Selected* (2020)

SAVING
our
SONS

SAVING
our
SONS

Raising Black Children
in a Turbulent World

MARITA GOLDEN

CORAL GABLES

Cover Design and Art Direction: Morgane Leoni

Cover Photos: Tatiana Katsai | Prostock-studio | liderina | stock.adobe.com

For permission requests, please contact the publisher at:

Mango Publishing Group

2850 S Douglas Road, 4th Floor

Coral Gables, FL 33134 USA

info@mango.bz

For special orders, quantity sales, course adoptions and corporate sales, please email the publisher at sales@mango.bz. For trade and wholesale sales, please contact Ingram Publisher Services at customer.service@ingramcontent.com or +1.800.509.4887.

Saving Our Sons: Raising Black Children in a Turbulent World

Library of Congress Cataloging-in-Publication number: 2021952510

ISBN: (p) 978-1-64250-893-2, (e) 978-1-64250-894-9

BISAC category code FAM043000, FAMILY & RELATIONSHIPS / Life Stages / Teenagers

Printed in the United States of America

This book is for my son, Michael, with thanks for

growing with me, for the generosity of his spirit,

and for allowing me to reveal his life to others

as the gift I have always known it was.

"The strongest lesson I can teach my son is the same lesson I teach my daughter: how to be who he wishes to be for himself. And this means how to move to that voice from within himself, rather than to those raucous, persuasive, or threatening voices from outside, pressuring him to be what the world wants him to be."

—Audre Lorde

"No black mother grows up in this city or any city without fearing for her son...No black mother doesn't fear. I don't think a black person can get away from it."

—Sylvia Snowden (mother of Malik Butler, who was murdered on a Washington, DC, street corner)

TABLE OF CONTENTS

FOREWORD

I met Marita Golden years ago when I was a reporter for the *Washington Post*. At the time, I was learning my way around Washington, DC. Marita moved among a flourishing group of Black writers in the city. In our encounters at cultural events around town and through reading her work, I saw Marita's passion for exploring the human condition, not only as a writer, but also as a world citizen.

I had been a fan of Marita's work since reading her first book, *Migrations of the Heart*. It was a searing account of her marriage to a Nigerian man and her subsequent relocation with him to the Motherland. In her four years living in Nigeria, she birthed a son and grew to appreciate an experience that most African Americans only dream of—living in a nation where Blackness is the norm. In *Migrations of the Heart*, Marita also chronicled the cultural and gender-related clashes with her husband that ultimately doomed her marriage and drove her to return to the United States.

It was apparent from *Migrations* and the books that followed that Marita's work as an artist reflects a drive to examine issues and seek answers to some of Black Americans' most pressing concerns. So it came as no surprise when her focus landed on her young son who, as a young Black male, inherited the dubious distinction of being labeled an endangered species in America. This book, *Saving Our Sons: Raising Black Children in a Turbulent World,* is the story of how Marita, then a single mother, set out with a fierce determination to raise an African-American boy in a country hostile to his very existence.

There is an obvious irony that made *Saving Our Sons* seem like an extension of *Migrations of the Heart*: Marita was struck by the fact that in Nigerian society, sons are held in high esteem. In America, however, the opposite is true. Black males are generally devalued and often treated as cogs in a nefarious school-to-prison-pipeline, where sizeable head counts bring vast profits on the New York Stock Exchange.

Year after year, the data about Black boys' prospects in life yields distressing news: Black boys are more likely than their white peers to be expelled from school. Black boys are more likely than others to be committed to detention centers for juvenile infractions. Homicide is a leading cause of death among Black males under the age of twenty-one.

Marita, faced with such a daunting reality, squarely confronted the probabilities of what might happen if she failed to help her son, Michael, navigate the pitfalls that awaited him, not only in the mean streets, but also in virtually every white-run institution that he would encounter over the years as he tried to find his way in America.

For me as a Black man, *Saving Our Sons* resonated in ways that are deeply personal. In a sense, I represent the embodiment of the nightmare that Marita hoped to avert in raising her son. I wrote about my journey in my autobiography, *Makes Me Wanna Holler: A Young Black Man in America.* I chronicled my passage from being a smart kid in elementary school to a corner boy by the time I reached junior high. Before all was said and done, I had shot a man in the chest at point-blank range and later committed an armed robbery that resulted in a twelve-year prison sentence.

As Marita noted in *Saving Our Sons*, such tragedies don't exist in a vacuum; they impact entire families and often sweep like cyclones through whole communities. I eventually managed to recover from my travails, but not before inflicting a great deal of collateral pain on my family and on others.

Saving Our Sons resonated with me for another reason as well. In Marita's story I came to better understand my own mother's anguished attempts to save me from the streets, from the system, and from myself. For all her maternal love and effort, my mom lacked the skills and vocabulary to forge the tough, often awkward conversations between parents and children that are so vital. Conversely, Marita forced herself to push beyond her comfort zone and engaged her son in discussions that challenged distorted schoolyard notions about sex, violence, manhood, and more that competed for space in his head. Additionally, she sought the help of experts and regular people whose lived experiences might offer critical insights on Black boys. And she enlisted the aid of the proverbial "village"— people in her community who could help reinforce positive images and messages.

Saving Our Sons is not some sterile account from an academic theorizing from the relative safety of the ivory tower. This is a deeply passionate account from a Black woman reporting from the front lines of a struggle that strikes at the very heart of Black survival.

In this book, Marita reminds us why every Black parent should be vigilant and intentional in considering how to steer young

Black boys—and girls as well—through the precarious passage to adulthood.

Saving Our Sons is disturbingly relevant in this, the twenty-first century. It's a compelling read.

—NATHAN MCCALL, author of *Makes Me Wanna Holler: A Young Black Man in America*

AUTHOR'S PREFACE

I remember it like it was yesterday. The evening my son Michael, then in junior high school, asked the question that inspired this book. "Why would God let that happen?" he asked me, trying to hold back tears as he told me that a friend from his school had been shot and killed as he left a party. He was fifteen years old. This was the second friend he had lost to gun violence. It was 1993. Some Black mother's son in this year of our Lord 2022 is asking the same question.

I wrote *Saving Our Sons* not because I thought I could answer my son's question, but because I loved him, and words were the only tools I had to fashion a response to one of the most universal questions: "Why do terrible things happen?"

My son was growing up against the backdrop of the most violent years of the War on Drugs, which we now know (and knew even then) was a War on Black Communities, a time when it was easier for a young Black boy in many communities to sell drugs than graduate from high school. And even if he did graduate, he would look around and see his urban community filled with more cops than jobs, more abandoned buildings than recreation centers or safe affordable housing, bereft of the amenities that foster community—parks, grocery stores, health care. Black communities were defunded of hope. Sound familiar?

I wrote *Saving Ours Sons* to grieve the carnage along with my community. Back then, an average of 400 mostly young Black men a year were killing each other in major cities like the one I lived in Washington, DC. I wrote *Saving Our Sons* to connect with the chorus of concern, wisdom, and compassion that I knew still had a heartbeat where Black people lived, loved, and yes, died. I wrote *Saving Our Sons* to lift the voices of young Black men who had become, to many Americans, Black and White, anonymous statistics, part of a numbing daily death toll. I wanted to beat the drum that heralded life in the face of death. And I wanted to create a space where we could hear the voices of the mothers, fathers, teachers, mentors, sisters, and brothers of the Black boys we wanted to save, and the writers and activists working to create a world where they would be safe.

I was gratified and felt vindicated by the response to this book, which became a bestseller and staple of book clubs and university classes. In telling the story of my determination to save my son and enfolding it within the larger vision and hopes and dreams of others, I created and found community and offered community to others.

I write this introduction nearly thirty years later when the death of one Black man, George Floyd, reminded America how fraudulent our assertions of progress were. I write this as the names of Trayvon Martin and Tamir Rice haunt us, and so many others gird us daily to fight police violence and murder. I write this nearly thirty years later when we now know how little difference a Black president makes in the quest to make America the America of its vaulted mythology.

I recall while writing this book, wondering if I could write a book that would be relevant, that decades later, readers would find themselves in, and be transformed by. And so, I filled this book with as much love and as many fully realized people and voices, and asked as many tough, sometimes unanswerable, even unfathomable questions as I could. I wasn't writing to be nice. I was willing to leave blood on the page.

This is the story of how I loved and raised and tried to make my Black son strong and sensitive and keep him safe. I fell down. Often. But I got up. We fell down. Often. But we got up. This is not a how-to book. Rather, it is a "How I did one of the hardest things you can ever try to do" book, and with faith in yourself and the support of family and community and luck, do it well. Jesse Jackson urged us to keep hope alive. Every parent who loves their child or children knows those words as prayer, mantra, and instruction. You cannot raise a Black child in America and not be an optimist, no matter what.

We have to save our sons and our daughters at a time when old-school systemic racism is now shaped and enhanced by climate change, artificial intelligence, social media turbulence, and the relentless replay of "Black death at the hands of cops" videos and a new outburst of White backlash. In 1969, Gil Scott Heron sang that while people had no food to eat on earth, "Whiteys on the Moon." Now the destination is Mars. Still. And yet. We have to raise sons and daughters who will not be the meek inheriting the earth. We will fight for them all. We will raise them to fight for their place in the sun. They are our wealth. They are our future. We have always known our Black children's lives mattered.

CALLING MY NAME

At a corner table in an upscale restaurant heavy on redwood paneling, scented candles, and a retro sixties atmosphere, Elaine Ellis Comegys and I sat talking about sons. I was a visiting writer in residence at Antioch College in Yellow Springs, Ohio, where Elaine is an associate dean of students. At noon we had set out, walking leisurely from the nearby campus to this restaurant located in "downtown," an area that is really no more than a five-block strip of retailers which include a gourmet carryout place, a health food store, an art supply shop, a children's bookstore, and the town's only theater. Yellow Springs possesses a vaguely aging counterculture feel, and the town invoked in me fond memories of a time when my Afro hair was several inches thicker than the close, conservative natural I wore that day.

Ebullient and warm, Elaine had given me a capsule history of Yellow Springs, population 4,000, including its status as a stop on the Underground Railroad. In May 1993, the town was bucolic, lovely, and so safe that unlocked doors along the wide tree-lined, shaded streets were common. The most serious recent crime wave anyone could remember was one spawned by a serial bicycle thief.

Psychologically, I was a long way from Washington, DC, where I returned each Thursday evening to spend the weekend with my family. I would be spending a month at Antioch, teaching a workshop on autobiographical writing, and so during lunch that day, I gently grilled Elaine, in a sister-to-sister-on-a-white-campus way, to tell me everything she knew that I should know too. Over Elaine's pasta and my fish, we dredged up academic anecdotes. We had both spent much of our professional lives on historically white campuses, and so the revelations and headshaking lasted awhile. But by the time we ordered dessert, we were talking about sons, ours and everyone else's.

Elaine and I landed on the gritty shore of this topic, any resistance to it capsized by its inescapable pull on our emotions. For at that moment, it was the fate and the crisis of our sons that obsessed and engaged us. Whether we were talking about the schools, a drive-by shooting, the economy, rap music, or the Knicks versus the Bullets, we were really talking about our sons. We talked about them because if we had not yet lost them, we feared we would. And looking into each other's eyes, hearing the confusion in our own voices, we wondered who could tell us how to get them back.

Elaine recounted an incident involving a Black writer we both knew whose son was driving home one evening in their affluent, mostly white neighborhood outside New York City. Shortly before reaching home, the young man was stopped by two white policemen who had been following him and had signaled for him to pull over. When he stopped his car and the policemen approached him, they grilled the young man as to why he was in the neighborhood. His assertion that he lived six houses down the block was greeted with disbelief, brutal laughter, and threatened physical punishment. Then they ordered him out of the car and handcuffed him. In the process of roughing him up, the policemen injured the nerves in the fingers of the young man's right hand so badly that he suffered permanent damage. He only escaped arrest when his younger brother, studying in the living room, noticed the reflection of the twirling red lights on the picture window of their house. He then went outside to investigate and found his brother being held down against the hood of a police car by the two cops, still insisting that he was simply on his way home. Only when the young man's parents came to the scene was he released.

"She was devastated, as you can imagine," Elaine concluded with a weary sigh, stirring her coffee. Her gaze, like mine—which was reflected in her glasses—was confounded. "And when we talked a few days after it happened, she kept asking over and over, 'How could this happen to my son?' "

"There was no label on him certifying that he was educated, middle class, not a dangerous 'bad nigger,' " I said, the Rodney King tape flashing, quick and painful, through my brain. "And who knows, that probably would not have even mattered. His skin, that's the only label they saw."

Then I began an account of the day a group of boys with guns entered my son's junior high school and methodically searched classrooms looking for a boy with whom they wanted to permanently settle a score. My voice tensed at the memory of how calmly my son told my husband, Joe, and me of the incident over dinner, how proudly Michael detailed his early departure by a side entrance to avoid a stray bullet or the impending fight rumored to be scheduled for the park outside the school that afternoon. "How did it get so bad?" I asked Elaine wistfully. "What happened? How did we become the enemy too?"

We sat there, two educated, articulate women who prided themselves on their ability to navigate the tightrope stretched between the Black and the white worlds. Now that the talk of sons had started, we recounted one incident after another—the son of a friend caught in cross fire, the son of a cousin doing time in jail for selling drugs. Yet for all the verbiage exchanged that afternoon, we were unable to explain how we had arrived in this season of blood and ashes.

That was the spring I decided I would remove my son from public school in Washington, DC, and enroll him in a private boarding school outside Philadelphia, as much to save his life as to buy him a good education. And after a lifetime spent in the inner city, my husband was suddenly willing to look at houses in the suburbs when we decided we needed more space. Drug traffic, once banished from our street by a combination of neighborhood vigilance and police cooperation, had returned. My car was broken into and the radio stolen. We lived five blocks from Howard University, two blocks from the now-boarded-up Howard Theater, once a mecca for Black stars from Duke Ellington in the thirties to James Brown in the sixties. Now addicts and prostitutes congregated all day before the grim, battered shell that was all that remained of the theater. And two weeks before my residency at Antioch began, a murderer dubbed the "Shotgun Stalker," who had randomly killed four people in a neighborhood a mile from where we lived, was captured in a parking lot three blocks from our house.

That afternoon, as Elaine and I sipped our herbal tea and nibbled our chocolate mousse, and after we paid the bill and walked slowly, almost reluctantly, back to campus, homicide was the leading cause of death for young Black males. That reality sat, a visible, intruding ghost, in the restaurant with us, strode along the clean neat streets of Yellow Springs, lay in wait for us in our campus offices. That statistic, like so much else in Black life, is surrealistic, chilling, and outrageous. Somewhere between the fact that Black males are the prime victims of crime and violence and the false media-generated image that they are responsible as well for nearly all the crime in America lies the truth. But where and how do you find it?

As the mother of a Black son, I have raised my child with a trembling hand that clutches and leads. I am no slave mother, my sleep plundered by images of the auction block. I dream instead of my son slaying the statistics that threaten to ensnare and cripple him, statistics that I know are a commentary on the odds for my son, who isn't dead or in jail. And though I have paved a straight and narrow path for my son to tread, always there is the fear that he will make a fatal detour, be seduced, or be hijacked by a white or a Black cop, or a young Black predator, or a Nazi skinhead, or his own bad judgment, or a weakness that even I as his mother cannot love or punish or will out of him.

And yet I say defiantly, "They are all my sons," the young prodigals as well as the boys who keep the faith of Black mothers and fathers. Over dinner a few weeks earlier, my friend Debra had described her new job as head of public relations for one of the largest hospitals in Washington. As part of her training, she had spent an evening in Medstar, the hospital's nationally known trauma unit. She was clearly shaken as she recalled, "The evening I spent in the trauma unit was hell. I felt so bad watching them bring in one Black male after another, shot in the arm, wounded in the chest. I watched them use electrodes to try to get their hearts going again. It's as if everything I'd read in the papers meant nothing until I was in that room to see it up close."

Patty, a TV producer, shifted in her chair next to Debra and pronounced, with more precision and honesty than I could bear, "I've got a six-year-old boy, and I feel like I'm raising a target."

I am too smart and too skeptical to believe all the hype. I know that it is only a small percentage of males in the Black community who have planted this terror we feel. But no matter how I add the numbers and take the pulse of my neighbors and friends, I know that African Americans inhabit a literal and figurative space unlike anything in our previous experience.

At a party one night, a journalist friend proudly said, "Look at all those white kids who get drunk and speed to their deaths in the suburbs, or their fathers who wake up one morning and shoot the whole family. We've no monopoly on violence."

"Maybe not, but proportionately, we've got a monopoly on death," I nearly screamed at him. "My husband is a high school teacher in Washington. How many teachers in Chevy Chase or Montgomery County can say, like him, that over a dozen students they've taught have been killed?" I was suddenly too weary to talk to my friend about the emotional toll of all this on my husband and his fellow teachers, as well as on their students, who had witnessed kids snuffed out literally before their eyes.

I have used language to decipher and overcome politically and culturally imposed madness. I have used words to claim sporadic cherished moments of beauty, real and imagined. And because all Black boys, the ones on the six-o'clock news in handcuffs and the ones singing in the church choir, are my sons, the sons of my community and the sons of America, I began searching for them that spring. I looked for our sons with a hunger that took root when my father first told me about my ancestors who built kingdoms and survived cotton fields; on the day my own son was born; and when the Black-on-Black violence began in earnest. Maybe, I thought, if I write long and hard and strongly and bravely enough, I can save and protect my son and somehow bless the others. This moment, when intraracial violence and death undermine any possibility for progress and complicate easy definitions of *The Problem* and *The Solution*, is a new kind of Middle Passage. What will we look like, how will we sound, once we are spewed forth from the terrible hold of *this* ship?

• • •

A few weeks before I began my residency at Antioch, Dr. Joyce Ladner, then vice president for academic affairs at Howard University, arranged for me to give a reading and lecture at Howard. A veteran civil rights worker who dodged bombs and bullets working for the Student Non-Violent Coordinating Committee in her home state of Mississippi, a nationally known sociologist, and the mother of a son, Ladner and I have known each other professionally for over twenty years. I have always profoundly respected her ability to capture and translate the voices of our young, whether it was the too-often hushed voices of young Black girls captured in her groundbreaking first book, *Tomorrow's Tomorrow*, or the bravado of young Black males on Washington's embattled streets whom she wrote about in a series for the *Washington Post*. After reading from one of my novels and answering questions in the chapel, I walked with Ladner across the Howard campus. The students we passed wore dreadlocks, fades, naturals, wigs, cornrows, African kente cloth, blue jeans, miniskirts; they were the first generation of Black people able to be "Black" any way they chose. Watching them, I wondered if they knew how much their parents, uncles, aunts, and generations of grandparents had "paid" for them to stride across the campus of a school, one at once historic and financially beleaguered, with a confidence they couldn't imagine not possessing. I mentioned to Ladner that I had decided to send my son to a private boarding school. I told her this because I remained conflicted. As a product of DC's public schools, I still believed in the ideal of public education and was haunted by the notion that I was copping out of the struggle and the race in making this choice.

"My son has been in boarding school for the past four years. He graduates in June." She beamed proudly as we reached my car. "I believe firmly that they are a valuable option. And I wish more Black parents could send their kids away."

I was surprised by her response, but as we continued to talk, Ladner spoke as a sociologist who had studied and witnessed the horrific impact of violence and crime in the Black community. For Joyce Ladner, boarding schools were simply a way of protecting Black kids from streets meaner than anything she or I ever knew.

I asked her what the trade-offs had been in sending her son away to school. "The first trade-off is he's *alive*," she said emphatically, the statement so stunning and assured I was momentarily left breathless. I wondered how many white women who were a stone's throw away from the presidency of a major university feared so much for their sons' safety that they could make a similar statement.

A daughter of the South, an intellectual, a scholar, a "sister," and still possessed of a soft, lilting Mississippi accent, when she recalls growing up in Hattiesburg, her voice is wistful and yearning. Ladner said that one of the primary reasons she chose a boarding school for her son was because "I wanted him to have a safe place to grow up, and I wanted him to have a nurturing, supportive community like the Black community that raised me in Mississippi." We talked about how growing up in the segregated South had shaped expectations and relations between Black men and women.

"Every generation of Black women has experienced tremendous anxiety about keeping their men alive," she said. Her words forced me to remember how frequently Black women are and have been leaders in the community, often brilliantly, by default, unrecognized and unrewarded. Now with the murders leaving widows, mothers of fatherless children, women who will never have men to marry, we have become leaders by some insane, demonic design.

"We as women always had to learn how to protect our men from white society," she said, remembering growing up in the fifties when a Black man, Mack Parker, was lynched in Mississippi after being accused of raping a white woman. She was fourteen when Emmett Till was murdered. Ladner reflexively hugged her body, leaned in closer to me as the memories induced an ache so palpable in her voice that I felt it too. Her voice fading to almost a whisper, she said, "When those men were killed, my fear was for my brothers, my uncles. I was a young girl scared for the men in my family. I remember having nightmares that someone would come and take all the men away. Today it's not the Klan in white sheets that's coming, it's more likely to be another Black male. Black women are still afraid for their men."

Each generation of Black mothers has hoped our sons would indeed become and always be the "Strong Men" poet Sterling Brown wrote of, who, undaunted and unbowed by racism, "keep coming, keep coming." And of our sons we eternally ask, how will they live, will they succeed? They must deal with myriad dangers, all while seeking always to know really who they are.

Our sons are Thomas Carrington, Ladner's pride and progeny, who would enter Syracuse University in the fall. They are my son, Michael, gangly, in the grip of a thunderous adolescence, baby-faced and grimacing. They are modern-day Dred Scotts, three fifths of a man, but now with an Uzi; they are football players, scholars, and would-be astronauts; they are William Horton, dubbed "Willie" in the racist corrupt ads of the 1988 Bush presidential campaign. They are Mike Tyson, National Merit Scholars, and an inner-city Black male infant, his prospects already curtailed.

They are not valued, nor listened to. They are not the problem but a symptom of a society in decay and decline, a society that has always used the Black man, the Black woman, the Black child, to symbolize its worst impulses, its throbbing underside. I know that the Black man has always been endangered. And if he is endangered, so, too, are his sister, his wife, and his mother.

Joyce Ladner and I represented the supposed realization of "equality" in the lives of contemporary African Americans. Yet our ascent into realms declared off-limits to our parents merely sharpened our ability to recognize the multitude of forms that institutional racism takes and its persistence. We were both women who saw whatever success we achieved in the white world as a tool to aid communities we were a part of no matter where we chose to live.

In several conversations over the weeks that followed my reading at Howard, Ladner and I talked about the complex equation that had produced this awful time. During one of our most wrenching dialogues, Ladner assessed the civil rights movement of which she was a part, saying, "There was a sense in which we wanted nice houses, decent schools, good neighborhoods so badly, and who could blame us, that we were willing to trade the good things in our community, the traditions, the beliefs, that were valuable in order to integrate." While Ladner was justifiably proud of the myriad social changes she had literally been part of creating, like many veterans of the civil rights movement with whom I had spoken, she now questioned the single-minded push for integration at the expense of protecting and enhancing Black businesses and the other institutions in the African-American community that had managed to serve us during segregation. Ladner's impassioned analysis represented not an attempt to mythologize an often unjust past; rather, her words symbolized a longing for a coherent present and future to give to our children.

At one point, she asked rhetorically, "What do we have to give our children now?" As we talked, I thought of the burgeoning and increasingly intense interest among middle-class African Americans in Afrocentric ideas, books, clothing, and styles. Men and women who worked in corporate America, calling institutions like Xerox and IBM "high-tech plantations," celebrated Kwanza, flocked to hear Nation of Islam head Minister Louis Farrakhan, gave their children African names. Yet hadn't we done this before in the sixties, sprouting naturals, wearing dashikis, fighting for Black studies, deigning and deciding to call ourselves "Black" with pride? And even in the 1920s, hadn't Marcus Garvey tapped into the best and brightest of our community to create a movement and an organization that were initially far-reaching, even though they are now erased from the books our children read? Weren't there "race men" and "race women" before? Yet each generation discovers, debates, dissects, and challenges the question of identity as if our race and our history were questionable propositions rather than undeniable facts.

Ladner concluded that this double consciousness, which we know both from the minutiae of our lives as well as from the pages of Du Bois's *The Souls of Black Folk*, is draining and sometimes killing our spirits. So often in the public and private discourse over integration, neither Blacks nor whites have assumed that African Americans brought anything of value to the process that would enhance white lives and world views. We came to the table as beggars, and even in three-piece suits and armed with honorary degrees, we are still scrambling for crumbs. We know that in our hearts. And so do our children.

And as the nation's economy is buffeted by such imperatives as "downsizing," increased computerization (which makes human hands obsolete), the influx of immigrants (who have taken over minimum-wage jobs that Black men once supported families on), and middle-class whites forced to take blue-collar jobs, where is there a job for my son? The trickle-down effect of misery fills street corners in the Black community with men who have never held a legitimate job. Work is available, but not enough for Black men who are unable to fill out a job application form even after graduating from high school, and who, because they are Black and male, instill fear and trembling in every white person in the company, from the receptionist to the head of personnel.

My son will know how to complete a job application. I will see to that. He will know how to stand with the right mixture of confidence and politeness as he enters an office suite, and he will know how to sell himself and his abilities articulately. But in an economy under siege and tunneling toward an ever-widening gap between rich and poor, employed and unemployed, what difference will that make? There will be fewer positions where a Black face will be tolerated. His confidence alone may instill more fear in the white man or woman who does the hiring and firing than a .38 pressed against their neck.

One evening, watching a Black politician on television—noting his smooth mastery of the jargon of intellectual and political discourse, his ease in the face of his interrogator, his regurgitation of the shallow doublespeak American politicians render so well—my husband, Joe, laughed, saying, "You know, I see now why whites are scared. If we turned off the picture, we'd think this guy was white. Hell, we can even beat them at that." With a shake of his head, he concluded, "They know if they level the playing field, it's over."

And so, my son may never inhabit a street corner as hustler or drug dealer, but he will have to be three times as good to get a job an "average" white man claims on the basis of genes alone. Affirmative action has put only a nick in the surface of that stony reality.

Considering the psychological circles we march in generation after generation, and the global and national economies we are victimized by, is it any wonder that in our communities the "drug boys" are major employers? We don't make the guns or import the dope, but despair and neglect motivate scarred, tremulous, even greedy hands to reach for crack vials. Yet who cares if 75 percent of the users are white? The drug boys introduce a level of fear, mayhem, and insecurity into the Black community that poisons relations between neighbors, lowers property values, and cheapens the meaning and essence of human life. Maybe it is true, as the popular slogan asserts, that we don't import the drugs or make the guns, but too many of our sons choose to reach for them.

Still, in the end and in the beginning, we can choose. Our sons and daughters must know that. Most of our sons do not sell drugs or brand their presence onto the surface of our memory through violence or mayhem. All of our sons need to recognize their lives as a memorial to the often graceful survival of African Americans who preceded them. Our sons must know that their lives belong to, and are claimed by, us all, and so they matter. Life has always mattered in the African-American community. Sometimes life—its potential, its bitter taste, its laughter ground into and alchemized by the ashes, its relentless hope—was all we had.

And so it is life that is the quest now. I want my son to grow up to be smart, productive, and content. But like every Black mother I know, I want my son, mostly, to live. White mothers insist, "I worry about my son too." And well they should. For while I seek to protect my son's life, any progressive, concerned white mother must strive to raise her son to resist and reject the legacy of his father. White mothers must raise their sons to welcome the necessary sharing of power, resources, and the world. White boys have to be taught to care whether my son lives or dies.

Michael is an Aquarius child, born on Valentine's Day like his maternal grandmother, who died seven years before his birth. At fifteen, he is five feet eight, nearly as tall as his father, towering six inches over me. Caramel-colored, he possesses his father's small ears and high forehead. Yet everyone has said I "spat him out," he looks so much like me. I see it too, in the cheeks, the curve of his lips. Thumbing through the photo album that charted his growth and mine, I see as well what is his alone. There is the smile, radiant, aggressive, always ready for the camera. There is no holding back, no shyness or hesitation. That is not me, always a bit uneasy before the camera, unsure whether to pose or be myself. Where I have resisted the camera, my son embraces it with unexpected mugging just before the flash, and with an ease that says, "Of course you want a picture of me."

One summer when Michael was six, I traveled to Belgium to visit friends I had made the year before during a trip to Senegal. Michael remained behind with a friend for three weeks and then flew alone to join me. When I met him at Charles de Gaulle Airport, the stewardess, grinning and shaking her head in amazement, told me, "He was seated next to a businessman from Chicago; they talked nonstop almost the whole flight."

Maybe it is his ability to talk that is my endowment. I play with, shape, and transform words on paper. Michael is enamored of their sound—their music and rhythm manifested through speech. He loves to tell jokes, make puns; and to my dismay, year after year in school he earned distinction as the class clown. At eight, he started reading the sports page daily and over dinner produced a new multisyllable word two or three times a week.

Burdened with talents and gifts, Michael drew well early and naturally, impressing the teachers in the Saturday afternoon classes at the Corcoran Art School. He had a flair for cooking, was an agile, enthusiastic athlete, and, when interested, could master a subject quickly. The years before his adolescence now seem to have been an extended, auspicious gardening, the planting of the seed, the quiet, sometimes breathless tending, the praying for rain and hoping for sun. Then comes the breaking of the sod and soil. You wake up one morning and there it is, a seedling; there he is, an adult, a man.

That spring when I was searching for the souls, examining the lives, of young Black males, I was learning, often against my will, clumsily but insistently, to let go. And this feeling of letting my son go was as heady and intoxicating as holding him tight in my arms, tucked beneath my breast. We had spent our lives together traveling toward the moments that awaited us, moments when he would turn his back on my beliefs, reject and then reclaim a value I had told him to honor; years when he would discover, abuse, and master free will, revel in his independence, yet thank God, he could always come home if he had to.

What if he was like me in the end, restless, searching, remaking myself like clockwork every few years by a new set of fantasies and goals? What if he ever said what I said to my mother when I was nineteen, brazen and so emboldened by the gospel of Black Power that I stood before her, hands on hips, and prophesied, "We won't make any progress until your generation dies off."

In the car one afternoon after Michael and I left a bookstore where I had had a friendly conversation with the owner about my newest book, a conversation during which I playfully lapsed into a fake Southern accent, Michael observed moodily as we drove off, "Why do you do that?"

"Do what?"

"Act different around white people. You and Joe. I've seen you. It's like you're tomming with them or something, it's like with them you're somebody else." The words doused me with surprise, and an embarrassment I couldn't explain.

Angrily clutching the steering wheel tighter, I said, "Nobody's tomming. What you call tomming is being friendly, that's all."

"Oh sure." My son's voice was derisive, surprisingly bitter. "You both act like they're something special. You're just normal in a Black store or restaurant. You're not fake there, why?"

How was I to tell him that despite our dinner table conversations about African history, capital punishment, war in Europe, and economic crisis in America, of which he is routinely a part—conversations in which intelligence and compassion make the morass manageable—the world is not black and white but often fuzzy, muted, and out of focus. I didn't tell him that when Joe receives an inquiry about the rooms in the rental property we own, if the prospective tenant is a woman, Joe insists that I come to the interview with him. As his wife, I have a vested interest in this business matter too. But my presence, with a ring on the fourth finger of my left hand, also defuses some of what makes white women afraid and Black women suspicious, the fact that Joe is a Black man. Was I to tell Michael, that day in the car, that the world feared him? Maybe he already knew.

Saving Our Sons

And so I said instead, "Michael, you don't know what you're talking about."

"Yes I do," he insisted defiantly.

"Being decent, even friendly, to whites isn't tomming, Michael, and I sure hope you don't think it is."

This anger, as fervent as a small brushfire beside me, represented my son's battle with the burden that his race has become in America. Perennially intractable, race as limit and as boundary had tied my son metaphorically in knots. This was how he would know one day that he was an adult. I had told him that he could be anything in a world where whites control everything political and material that matters. I had told him to respect himself, but my lectures about racism had perhaps instilled the suspicion that whites didn't deserve the respect he extended to himself. And, increasingly, I was lecturing him to be as careful around young boys who looked just like him as in the presence of white people who didn't. "Ambivalence" and "compromise" were words my son at fifteen could spell, perhaps even define. But they were words that had not yet tested his resolve or courage.

I was still dazed, flushed by the emotions Michael's accusation had unearthed. And as we turned onto our street, I heard him mutter again through clenched teeth, "When I grow up, I'll never be a tom."

I said nothing more, for I was letting go of him and it was messy and scary. He was letting go of me, and I wondered how that felt.

• • •

Once, we talked about everything. Now it seemed so hard. Was it because my son was a teenage Black male, and so, as a result, so much of what I felt compelled to say other than "I love you" was warning, caution, and critique? For Michael, the line of demarcation between child and adulthood was not a border but a precipice. There was so much to tell and so much he had to know, so little time and so few situations within which to frame the conversation.

Michael has the soul of a bear in winter, for at night, he sinks not merely into sleep but into a hibernation that defies alarm clocks, my screams up the stairs to get up, even sometimes the smell of pancakes in the kitchen. Meeting my teenaged son in the hall at seven in the morning was like running into a man with evil on his mind in a dark alley.

When he took up residence in the bathroom, his ever-deepening voice, resonating like a talking drum, filled the hallway with the latest hot rap lyrics, uttered so quickly in a battered staccato that they whizzed by like bullets ricocheting off the walls.

Allegedly awake, walking as slowly through the house as if each step had been choreographed for special effect, he would enter the kitchen wearing a shirt two sizes too big (he was in style), jeans, unlaced sneakers, a jacket inappropriate for the weather outside. Looking into the refrigerator (his favorite pastime), he'd grab a Sprite. "Not in this house," I'd say, lifting the soda from his hand and placing a glass of orange juice there instead. Apparently, breakfast was uncool, for it required five minutes of debate to get him to eat a slice of toast.

No time to talk now. I would hustle him out the door, fuming as I watched him walk as though he was on a picnic in the woods, not as though already late, toward the subway and school.

After school, when homework was done, he'd go outside, talk to boys on the block. I was cooking dinner once when he trooped in with two friends, Leonard and Calvin. No video games on school nights, no TV until after dinner, so the three boys sat in the living room trading baseball cards. While I moved between kitchen and dining room, it was Michael's voice I heard most as he regaled his two friends with anecdotes, statistics about players and games. With Michael's edgy yet playful laughter filling the house, he stood up before the other two to imitate a play, sprawled over the couch one minute, edged closer to Leonard the next to sell him a card. With his peers, he was natural and easy, and soon all three were laughing, joking. Michael was ringmaster of the event.

And yet he was comfortable being alone. Saturday afternoons he might spend in his room drawing, reading magazines, playing video games, and staunchly resist the call of friends to join them. As an only child, he learned to entertain himself, feeling perhaps that his thoughts possessed more integrity than the lure of tales others might weave. Of all the traits my son possesses, I admire most in him this independence. More than anything, I would wish for him a fierce loyalty to being who he is, who he wants to be—if need be, by himself.

Over dinner, finally there was time to talk—but not always of the most important things. Skillful mastery of the mundane, I had learned, was part of parenting too. With Joe teaching math three nights a week at Armstrong Adult Education Center, Michael and I could be alone. We talked about the news, school, family, friends. There were still times, even now, when we flashed back to an intimacy that I missed and he had not yet completely forsaken.

Many of our most memorable conversations took place in the car, driving to karate lessons or art classes, or on weekends when the three of us often headed to the mall for a movie. The car was where we talked about sex. I'd found a condom on the floor of Michael's bathroom the day before. The unused yellowish device, limp and harmless in my palm, symbolized all the "official" lectures about sex that Michael had endured. In the fifth grade, he brought home a form from school for me to sign giving permission for him to take the sex education class. I had bought a human anatomy book for children for him when he was five. In eighth grade, there were lectures on sexually transmitted diseases in health class. He was vaguely aware, I suspected, of the nuts and bolts and the mechanics of intercourse from all this, which equated the act with dissecting a frog or building a chair.

A few minutes into our drive—on this day, to the dentist—and after mentally sifting through the two dozen ways I had considered broaching the topic, I finally asked, "Where'd the condom come from?" I strove to balance nonchalance and concern, so as not to tip the always precarious balance we now seemed to maintain against full disclosure. Michael said he'd been given the condom during a lecture about AIDS prevention at the all-male after-school program he'd attended. During the lecture, the boys had practiced putting a condom on a banana. I was not certain, however, that this meant they would put it on themselves.

"Who'd you say gave the AIDS lecture?" I asked, stopping at a red light. I wondered if I sounded as wired to Michael as I did to myself.

"Some lady from the city health department."

"Oh." Uncomfortable pause. "You probably knew a lot of what she talked about, I guess, huh?" I said, wondering how much he really knew, realizing that we'd had a couple of brief conversations about sex, hit-or-miss, hit-and-run efforts, but nothing like the in-depth cozy dialogues with your child the manuals advise.

"I knew some of it." He shrugged, opening the glove compartment and reaching for a stick of gum. The sound of the gum wrapper being squashed by his fingers was the only sound in the car. I turned on the radio for support and asked, "What didn't you know?"

"Well, like about the different kind of condoms, the best ones to use, and how even when you do other stuff you can get AIDS."

"Other stuff?" I turned to look at Michael and he was gazing out his window, taking refuge in the sight of familiar streets.

"What other stuff? You mean like drug use?"

"I knew that," he said to the window, his voice nearly muffled.

"Well, what other stuff?"

"Like oral sex." Michael turned to face me now, his gaze gauging the effect of his words.

"Ooooooooohhhhhhh, oral sex," I said, as though I had never heard the words before in my life. Hoping to regain control, I said, "So much of what everyone tells you about sex, Michael, is clinical, and it's easy to lose the real meaning of it." I was back on solid ground, entrenched in the touchy-feely, slightly intellectual mode I handle best. But was he listening?

"I mean, what sex is really about is two people who respect and care for each other, and sex is an expression of that. You shouldn't, for example, have sex to prove anything. And there are so many emotions involved in having sex. Your body may feel ready, but you may not in fact be prepared, mentally I mean."

"A lot of my friends say they've had sex."

"A lot?"

"Sure. But I know they haven't. I can tell. When we're together, they say stuff like 'Yeah man, it was so good. She didn't want me to stop. I was killing her.' "

I sat imagining the young boys who entered our house to play video games and bicycle down to the mall talking like this. I nearly hit a pedestrian crossing the street.

"Does that make you want to have sex?"

"No. Not just because they did."

"Have you had sex?"

There, I've said it, I thought. Suddenly I felt lighter. I could even breathe again.

"No, I didn't have sex yet," he said calmly, but clearly anguished, angry, and embarrassed that I had asked.

"Well, don't rush into it. Don't do it with just anybody. You've got plenty of time."

"Okay, mom. Okay."

"Your body isn't something you share with just anybody. It's special, remember that."

"Okay, mom. Okay."

I was breathlessly issuing orders, pleading for sanity and safety. Relieved he hadn't had sex yet, yet still scared knowing one day he would, I added, "And when you do, use a condom."

"Okay, mom. Okay," he said gently, placing a hand on my arm as we arrived at our destination.

I turned to look at him, imagining an AIDS-emaciated face staring back at me, recalling the article I'd read chronicling the increase in AIDS among Black youth, citing it as a close second to homicides in some cities as the leading cause of death.

"If you don't ever want me to have sex, just say so." Michael grinned, brazenly sarcastic.

"Michael, I just want you to be careful," I told him, smiling as I attempted to be less grim. In the wake of this assurance, I thought, as I do every day, although I did not say it, "And I just want you to live."

Growing up in the Black community in the fifties in Washington, DC, I was part of the last generation that, across income and class lines, benefited from a pervasive network of family and kinship ties that effectively met the needs of mothers and children. In the summer, I visited my maternal grandmother, Molly Reid, in Greensboro, North Carolina. I recall my grandmother as a strict and often stern woman of silences, yet a woman who quickly garnered respect and attention when she chose to speak. These annual summer sojourns joined me to family; they fixed in my consciousness that I was a Golden, but also that I was a Reid.

Summer in Greensboro meant driving with my cousins Bunny and Fairdon and their mother, Aunt Janey, to visit her mother, "Ma Head," and eating fried chicken and apple pie or whatever Ma Head had on the stove while the two women talked on the front porch. Greensboro nights were tranquil, the darkness deep and solemn. My cousin Debra would come down from New York in the summer sometimes too, and we'd spend evenings chasing fireflies on Granny Reid's front lawn and imprison them in glass jars. In those summers, Greensboro, like all of the South, was rigidly segregated. Not for several more years would Southern Black college students assault institutional racism by sitting in at counters at Woolworth's or freedom riding their way on Greyhound and Trailways buses across the South. But for me as a Black child, the community of which I became a part for eight weeks each year was cocoon and buffer. The world beyond was racist and cruel, but my grandmother, my aunts, and my uncles all conspired to protect my cousins and me from the destruction that that world sharpened like a precise tool. And so Greensboro was my uncle Robie's effusive, effervescent laughter, his jokes and teasing. I did not know then that he was an alcoholic, I just loved the drenched gleam in his eye and his determination to handle anything that came along with a rakish, irresistible smile. When my uncle Robie died when I was a teenager, I used the memory of his laughter to defeat the terrible images of the alcoholism that had induced his death.

When I was very young, my mother's women friends often cared for me. And as I grew, I could call on a host of aunts and "play mothers," babysitters, birthday and graduation rememberers, and I'm-mad-at-Mama-so-I-need-to-talk-to-you-'cause-I-know-you-won't-tell-her-what-I-said confidantes.

In raising my son, however, I was unable to call on this kind of support. The education I had achieved endowed me with a mobility and appetites that loosened family ties. The Black family, mine and everyone else's, responding to the effects of integration and other social patterns, became less monolithic and communal.

But it was the deaths of my mother (of a cerebral hemorrhage when I was twenty-one) and my father (of a heart attack when I was twenty-two) that severed my sense of connectedness to human forces much larger than myself. Their nearly simultaneous demises abruptly launched me on a persistent, often relentless search for community, a sense of family, place, and roots.

My mother, Beatrice Lee Reid, was an extraordinary self-made, self-possessed woman who left Greensboro as part of the Great Black Migration of the late 1920s. She settled in Washington, DC, where, within a few years of her arrival, she had parlayed her modest earnings as a domestic worker, along with her penchant for winning at the "numbers game," into ownership of several boardinghouses.

I was born, much to my mother's surprise, when she was forty-two years old. I know now that I became a writer as much because I was an obedient child as because I could not help it. For it was my mother who had proudly watched me recite my poems in school pageants and plays, who had seen me at the age of ten mailing letters to the editor of the *Washington Post*, and who looked at me one afternoon across the kitchen table, where she stood rolling dough for biscuits, and said, "One day you're going to write a book."

I sat at the table, thumbing through a copy of *Little Women*, and was so stunned by my mother's declaration that I stammered out, "Oh, Mama, I couldn't ever do that." I told her this, I, the daughter who spent whole summer days in the attic reading as though her life depended on it, the daughter who walked past neighbors without speaking, neighbors she hadn't seen because at that moment a story was taking shape in her head. Ignoring my protests, my mother continued, embellishing what struck me then as an entirely fanciful proposition. "In fact, before it's all over, you probably will write more than one book," she said, smiling slyly, utterly pleased with herself and totally convinced of the certainty of her prediction.

I remember rising from the table, frightened and on edge. I fled the kitchen. My mother's words were so laden with the promise of power, the possibility of miracles, that I was literally trembling. I was twelve years old and my mother had baptized me. She could have told me I'd grow up to be someone no one would ever listen to. She told me instead that I was destined to write stories that would be hard to resist.

I had seen the house my mother was born in, once, during my annual pilgrimage to North Carolina. It was a weather-beaten, run-down shotgun shack, abandoned but still standing. The day my mother anointed me, however, we sat in a three-story house of twelve rooms, with oriental carpeting, a Zenith stereo, and gilt-edged mirrors. This was my mother's house. So I knew that a woman could become a "self-made man," could become who she needed and wanted to be. Still, I was astounded that day, thought my mother was crazy. Six years later, my mother gave me a subscription to the *New York Times* for my eighteenth birthday. I was entering American University in the fall and had talked about becoming a journalist. My mother wanted to initiate me into the language I would need to begin learning how to speak.

Because she gave birth to me in middle age, with each passing year my mother repeated like a litany, "I just want to live long enough to see you graduate from high school." Her large, always somehow mournful eyes appeared to miss me even as she spoke. When I graduated from Western High School, she amended her wish, saying, "I just want to live long enough to see you graduate from college." But she died in my junior year.

If my mother gave me the charge to write, it was my father who schooled me, rigorously, consciously, and unconsciously, in how to tell a story. My father, Francis Sherman Golden, was a very dark, intensely proud Black man. Partially named after the Union general who burned Atlanta during the Civil War, my father was abundantly, shamelessly charismatic, and he, like my mother and my son, was an Aquarius, loquacious and charming. My father spun for me tales of legendary figures from Black history. Hannibal, Cleopatra, and Frederick Douglass peopled my bedtime stories. My father was "Afrocentric" long before the term was coined. I learned from my father that a good story involves drama, conflict, change, growth. And years later, when I wrote about my parents, I envisioned them grand, heroic, larger than life, because in a sense they were, but also because with his voice, my father had etched for me the thrilling deeds of men and women who had transformed themselves and the lives of others. Estranged from his only son from a previous marriage, who was fifteen years older than I, my father raised me as though I were his favored son, taking me for rides in his taxicab as he ferried passengers all over the city, allowing me to follow him into gambling joints, sitting with me at night in the summer on the front stoop, or before the fireplace in winter, explaining politics, history, the entire world from his point of view. My father taught me that I was worth talking and listening to.

These were the parents I lost before they had a chance to watch me take on the world they promised me was and could and should be mine. These were the grandparents my son was denied.

What would my parents have thought when I fell in love with and married a young Nigerian architectural student and went to live in Lagos with him? As much as I wanted to create a family of my own, I wanted to somehow "recapture" my parents through marriage.

It was in Africa that I became a mother. I had married into a large Yoruba extended family whose members included my US-educated husband, Femi, and other similarly educated cousins and brothers and sisters, as well as family members who were barely literate. The Ajayis were a clan of strivers and upwardly mobile achievers. My husband's great-great-great-grandfather had been a member of the royal court of a Yoruba king, and the entire family wore this genealogical inheritance like a cherished mantle.

My son was named, as custom allowed, by his grandmother: Akintunde Babatope—and also at my insistence, Michael. His first name means "The spirit of the father returns"; all the male names in the family carry "Akin" as a prefix. Babatope means "Praise be to God."

In my husband's culture, when a woman gave birth to a child, she gave up her name to be called "Mama [name of child]." It was a society in which fertility was worshiped, fecundity prized. So as a male, my son was not just welcomed but treasured. His gender bestowed honor and legitimacy on me, status on his father. My first child had also been a boy, but he had died three days after his premature birth at seven months. And so Michael held within him some part as well of the brother who had preceded him.

To celebrate the birth of our son, friends and family gave us monetary gifts totaling the equivalent of fifteen hundred dollars, and we held an elaborate naming ceremony which began with an old family friend acting as a priest addressing everyone gathered. He poured a libation, sprinkling gin onto the floor to honor the Ajayi ancestors, believed always to be present. My son was officially named as child of us all, belonging not just to his father, Femi, and to me but to all the Ajayi clan. Then the priest reached into several bowls placed on a nearby table and dabbed a bit of each ingredient (honey so life would be sweet, water so he would be great like the sea, salt so he would know that life is difficult) onto my son's tongue and mine and Femi's. After that, the bowls were passed around the room for all who had gathered to share. Later that evening, one of Femi's older brothers sat with me and celebrated the birth of my son by telling me the history of the Ajayi clan, acting as griot and charging me to tell the story to Akintunde one day.

I had wanted family, and it was family that I now had. But I had come to Nigeria a feminist and was confronted again and again by the regressive roles and treatment of women in my ádopted country and what they portended for me and for my son. My mother-in-law, a feisty, quick-witted, intelligent woman, had worked long hours on her husband's rubber plantation, had sold foodstuffs in the market, and had borne three sons, two of whom she had helped send to study abroad. My sister-in-law helped my husband's brother work his way through school in London. She was a kind of human dynamo, running her household and her stall in the local market with breathtaking efficiency. Both these women and others like them were valued among the Yorubas because they worked hard and bore sons. Among the Yorubas, a woman was encouraged to be financially independent and to have a trade of her own.

But the journalism classes I taught at the University of Lagos were overwhelmingly male because it was considered a waste to send a girl to college. I knew that female children were still subjected to clitorectomies, a form of genital mutilation that no one I asked seemed willing or able to explain. Polygamy still flourished; it was respected and practiced widely. The few single Nigerian women I had met could not imagine themselves remaining single. One woman, a reporter for the country's most respected newspaper, told me, "There would be no place for me in my society as a single woman. I would not count, would not even exist in the minds of my family and friends."

Here was a country that was one of the largest, most populous, and most influential in Africa. My son was by birth a member of a tribe whose culture was deep, rich, and complex. We lived in a nation where the head of state was Black, where when I boarded a plane, the pilot was Black, and where all the women possessed my hue or some variation of it, as well as my broad hips. I saw some resonant, primal part of myself everywhere I looked. And I wanted this racial inheritance for my son.

But what was the inheritance really? Corruption in Nigeria was rampant, the oil wealth was being wasted, and I knew that a group of men could meet around a wood-paneled table in a bank in Luxembourg or London and, with a show of hands or their signatures on a piece of paper, cripple or completely destroy the economy of the country. Nigeria was large and populous, but like every country in the Third World, it was a nation of paupers. Its popular culture was schizoid, with young people who used bleaching creams on their skin and listened to American music, but visited juju men in moments of doubt. Half the population was still illiterate, and every attempt at democracy had been sabotaged by the military. What really was my son a part of? His heritage and inheritance here were as conflicted and bittersweet as the ones he would have had if born in America.

When I left my husband four years after I had arrived in Nigeria and a year after my son's birth, my departure had more to do with emotional incompatibility than with politics. Yet the expectations Femi and I brought to our union had been shaped by how we had seen men and women love one another in the cultures that had produced us. Culture and mythology are political; Nigeria taught me that.

Our separation and subsequent divorce were bitter and recriminatory; for me, they launched a long period of paranoia and fear that Femi would attempt to take Michael from me forever (a fear stoked by threats made repeatedly in the heat of anger and by my knowledge that in the Nigerian legal context, my son, no matter what a court in the United States said, "belonged" to his father). The decision to restrict Michael's access to his father and, for long periods of time, not to allow his father to know where we lived was a painful, difficult one. It was made, however, based on my knowledge of how Femi handled anger and frustration. He had never really trusted me with his deepest feelings. How could I trust him with our son?

Black fathers, actually and legendarily, have often been the psychological missing link in the African-American community. But I had known and loved my father; he was present in my life, a commanding, impossible-to-ignore influence, even after my mother left him. The specter of the shiftless can't-be-trusted-never-around-when-you-need-him-can't-or-won't-respect-or-protect-his-woman Black man harnesses and corrupts so many Black women's expectations of the men who are their fathers, husbands, lovers, friends, and sons.

And so the absence of my son's father in his life was not merely my own private tragedy. It was, in my eyes, a failure of community as well. For my divorce and my estrangement from my son's father pushed Michael and me closer to the starting line of a race we would have to run already crippled. After my parents' separation, I had witnessed how they forged forgiveness and respect from the remains of a passionate, difficult union. But I wanted to give my son the ideal family even though I knew it did not exist. I wanted him to have a father in his life, despite the statistics that informed me there were eighty-nine Black men for every one hundred Black women. Was that why I married an African? Maybe, I thought in my moments of greatest doubt, we can't escape history. But still, I tried. Many days I did. I never would have imagined myself as a mother who willfully denied a child of mine his father.

The decision I made out of fear brought order to my life but little peace of mind. The prayers I mouthed each night, prayers that my son never heard, asked to know when I could reach out to a man I had once loved and now did not trust. When the answer came, it was my son who showed me the way.

• • •

For five years after returning to the United States from Nigeria, Michael and I lived in Boston. I chose the city because I had developed a friendship with a woman from Boston while she was an exchange student studying at the University of Lagos. When I wrote her that I was returning to the States, she had agreed to help me get settled. After teaching for three years at the University of Lagos, I also thought I could easily find a teaching job in a city long considered an educational hub.

In the first years following my return, the contradictions of my life were vivid and almost insane. I was a writer whose words and thoughts thrust me into the public domain. Yet, quite frankly, in the years after my divorce, I became a woman who was hiding her son from his father. When I broke off communication with Femi, on several occasions Ajayi relatives resident in this country nearly found us. But they never quite did. This was my life, one I often felt doomed to live forever.

In Boston I was totally unprepared for the ethnic and racial balkanization I found. It was 1979, and the bruising, often violent battle over busing that had scarred the city's image still left smoke literally tingeing the air. White cab drivers refused to take me to my Roxbury apartment after dark. I was not welcome in "Southie," the Irish-Catholic enclave, the North End (Italians), or any part of Dorchester, where working-class whites predominated. For the first time in my life, as I searched for an apartment, I was openly, blatantly rebuffed because of my race.

The middle-class Blacks I met were insular and snobbish and too often tried to claim their ancestors came over on the Mayflower too. And yet the racial intolerance of the city was countered by a thriving arts and theater scene and some of the best museums in the country. This provided a partial salve for the sting of living in the most racially primitive city I had ever known. The weather was as hostile as many of the people I met, for winter arrived arctic and cruel in October and didn't depart until April or May.

My first job was teaching at Roxbury Community College, then a struggling stepchild of the state system of higher education. Housed back then in a former convent, its decrepit interior was one of leaky ceilings and small, overcrowded classrooms. But the student body— mostly older, often fully employed Africans, Caribbeans, African Americans, and Hispanics, with a few Asians and whites tossed into the stew—was hardworking and motivated. I learned as much from my students from Eritrea and Trinidad as I taught them. My colleagues were, like me, often disgruntled over our relatively low salaries and the dismal state of the building. But dedication to the students was never in short supply.

Michael was a year old when we moved to Boston, and I collected a bumper crop of day-care horror stories. There was the day-care provider I found from a list of city-approved centers for children under two. Each day when Michael was brought home at six o'clock, moments after she sped off, he gazed mournfully at me for several moments as though to be certain that we were alone, his small body tensed, clearly on guard, and then burst into a tantrum, crying, screaming, releasing a rush of pent-up rage. My even-tempered son had suddenly become a volatile neurotic, fighting and kicking me as I hustled him from the front door upstairs to our apartment.

After three days of scenes like this, I made an unscheduled visit to the center and found that the owner had regimented the children so intensely that the toddlers in her care possessed the arch obedience of small robots. Michael, I soon saw, was rebelling against this strict regimen the only way he knew how.

The very best, most nurturing day-care provider my son ever had was ironically denied a license by the city because the space in her basement where her center was set up was ten feet less than required. But she loved all the children in her charge with an enthusiastic, unabashedly maternal fervor, and the children made developmental progress that was so rapid it seemed designed as her reward. This woman kept my son during the day for a year. I knew she was unlicensed; she had told me that up front. But because she was so obviously gifted in her approach to children, I took a chance. Then one snowy January morning Michael and I arrived at her house and found the door locked. I checked with a neighbor, who told me that the woman had gone to Florida the night before, having been tipped off by a friend who worked for the city that she was to be inspected and would be fined heavily if caught with children in her care.

My son and I were entirely dependent on the patience, concern, and training of strangers. The "day-care question," and how it was solved, determined whether or not I could concentrate on my work. It controlled my son's emotional development and the peace of mind of us both. And because the welfare of children remains at the bottom of this nation's priorities, neither my income nor my class guaranteed competent care for Michael. Unfortunately, all children in America possess an equal opportunity to be poorly cared for, indifferently nurtured, exploited, or abused.

• • •

When I was hired as a full-time member of the Department of Mass Communication at Emerson College, the job boosted my salary as well as our lifestyle and possibilities. I moved from Roxbury to the South End, then in the throes of a frenetic process of gentrification. It was a neighborhood where Blacks, whites, gays, yuppies, and Hispanics all lived side by side but rarely mixed. I enrolled my son in an excellent private nursery school on Newbury Street owned by a Black woman.

Home for us was the Piano Factory, an artists' community where spacious studio apartments were carved out of a building that had once actually been a piano factory. This apartment building was everything the city outside its doors was not. Here was a community. My neighbors were photographers, dancers, painters, artists, struggling and successful. They hailed from New York City and Bolivia, Greece and Oakland. A small art gallery on the first floor displayed the work of resident visual artists; our children played in a grassy courtyard that had swings and a sandbox and an area where parents could sunbathe.

Maybe fate and circumstance had denied my son his father, but I determined I would give him everything else. Weekends we made trips to the city's impressive Children's Museum. I bought season tickets to a children's theater company. Our neighbors were artists like Paul Goodnight, whom my son saw fill canvases with rich, vibrant colors, life, and people. Michael listened to Paul and me talk, over incense and herbal tea, about art and Black folk and our artistic ambitions.

By the time Michael was six, he had petted baby llamas in the San Diego Zoo and spent two weeks in Puerto Rico, where I sat watching him build castles in the white, shimmering sand and thought that just watching him beneath a Caribbean sun was as much as I would ever want or need. And when I yearned for Africa, even as I feared a return to Nigeria, we spent three weeks in Senegal, where he climbed onto the cannons that guarded the slave castle on Gorée Island and where we made Jamaican friends who lived in New York and artist friends who lived in Belgium. And there were occasional holiday visits to Washington, DC, to visit family there.

Yet I often felt overwhelmed, lonely. I worried about what would happen to my son if I died, resented the fact that as a single parent I was always on call. I got no vacations, and despite numerous friends, I often felt there was no one with whom I could share the fatigue, frustrations, or triumphs inspired by the life I lived with my son. Michael had never really seen me loving his father. What could he possibly remember of his first year of life, a year that marked both his birth and the painful, tortured end of my marriage? More than once I prayed that he remembered nothing, since I could recall nothing from that year that I wanted to hold on to except his birth. While I had several close platonic friendships with men I'd met in Boston, lovers were few and far between. What, I wondered almost obsessively, was Michael learning about love from watching me?

The headlines during these years were a foreboding, shrieking backdrop for my personal anxieties and fears as they asked "Single Parents: How Bad for the Children?" or predicted "Single Parent, Double Trouble," "Woe Is One, Two Parents Are Better, It Seems." The demographics of the Black community had changed dramatically since my childhood, a period in which children born out of wedlock or even living with one parent were more easily absorbed into the fabric of the community by extended families who provided mother and child with emotional and material support. Parents were living longer, retiring later, and were too busy with hobbies and interests of their own to serve as built-in babysitters. The infusion of drugs and guns and the accompanying violence into the Black community had created social problems so profound that even the strongest extended families were rendered incapable of answering the call of sons and daughters in need. Most of the women I knew raising children alone, even those who had parents to lend a hand, complained of feeling isolated, ignored, and misunderstood. And if you were a Black woman raising a male child, the Black community became a chorus of naysayers, assuming you were not up to the task of raising the kind of "man" the race needed to make progress, yet refusing to create institutional assistance that might make a difference. Everything and everybody, it seemed, conspired to convince me that I could not raise a boy who could become a healthy, productive adult. Men I dated entered my apartment and, watching Michael in a range of normal activities, critically concluded, like doctors examining a sick patient, "What he needs is a man in the house."

Yet I knew that generations of Black women had successfully raised male children who became decent, loving fathers and husbands and members of the community. And inevitably, along the way, the brightest of these boys sought out some coach, male teacher, deacon in the church, or uncle or friend for guidance and encouragement. Children know what they need and are often adept and skillful at finding it. In other cases, men stepped forward to help mothers mold the character of their sons.

I suffered moments of doubt and attacks of guilt as I raised my son, but most days I swallowed the guilt, pushed aside the doubts. I had neither time for them nor interest in allowing them to define my life. I plodded on, saying "yes" to me and my son even though the world gazed on skeptically, whispering "no" loud enough for me to hear.

For while I was raising a boy who would one day be a man, I was trying to raise a well-adjusted, loving, responsible human being whose yin and yang I wanted to balance. My son saw me get up and go to work every morning, felt me kiss him goodnight, and was in the presence, via my platonic friendships, of men who were capable and often accomplished. He got lectures on his history as an African American from me, watched my loyalty to my friends, bore my punishment when he deserved it, was served dinner every night at six, and was bought encyclopedias and video games.

Still, how would Michael judge, and remember, me? How would he see me in memory, as I tried to be mother and father too? As a Black woman raising my son alone, did I sometimes let him become for me the "good man" I feared I might never find? I was not supposed to have come this far; he was not supposed to have turned out so well. Because we were African American, pathology and defeat were assumed to be our mother/son legacy. How could I raise Michael against the odds, and with laughter and gentleness? In a world where whites assumed whiteness equaled the universal human experience, I had to teach my son that his race was not a crucible and that all the people whiteness tried to render invisible possessed beauty he must see, wisdom he should learn. And as his mother and on some days father too, I was afraid for him and for myself. I was lonely and confused. Yet the need to keep my son fed, clothed, and loved propelled me, stoked ambition, satisfied hunger.

The "rap" against Black mothers is that we spoil our sons and raise our daughters. Denied by past and current racism, lacking competent adult partners, we shower our sons with the affection we hunger for, overinvest ourselves emotionally in their dreams, all to live vicariously through them. This is the charge. But in a racist, patriarchal society, how else, it might be asked in response, are some Black women to be realized if not through sons—sons who even under siege can in full flower ascend in ways still denied to women? Mothers in cultures around the globe, not just in Black communities in Chicago or Detroit, invest their own denied ambitions in their sons. Only in a world where women's goals are not stunted will this equation no longer persist. Mothers often see fragile, ephemeral hope when they look at their daughters; they see rock-solid possibilities when they gaze at their sons.

But I didn't spoil Michael; I raised him, knowing it was just the two of us, envisioning him as a resource for his family, his people, and his planet. I raised my son fearing I was not enough, imagining neurosis, psychosis, incubating within his spirit because of his absent father, the father I chose to leave. I carried all this, and remnants of it still snag projections and plans. Black mothers have transformed the shouldering of pain and responsibility and regret into a cryptic art form.

I despised the term "single parent," for I knew that no one ever really raises a child alone. The challenge I faced as my son grew was to build a surrogate family that would meet our need for community and connections. The search and need for family were part of the reason I had married Femi. This time I turned to the church.

Through a friend who lived in the Piano Factory, I began attending a small, racially mixed Baptist church in the neighborhood. The intimate congregation numbered only a hundred members. I was assigned to a "small group" of eight members who initiated me into the church and introduced me to other members with whom I engaged in weekly Bible study. There was no official or unofficial dress code at this church, and the God who prevailed here accepted congregants in blue jeans, dreadlocks, shorts, or three-piece suits. Following the service, everyone gathered for dinner in the church basement and it was not uncommon for a homeless man or woman to break bread with us.

During each service, there was a period where congregants could simply stand to share problems for which they sought prayer or to reveal good news. Much of the most vibrant spiritual energy in this church flowed from the membership to the pastor and mutually among the congregants. In the placement of the pulpit (centered and on the same level as the pews), in its expressed and acted-upon spirit, the church deconstructed the minister as all-knowing patriarch and invested the membership with a sense of their own significant abilities to heal and to teach.

I became close friends with a white couple, Rudy and Sara Maxwell, who were leaders of my assigned "small group." As a child, Sara had lived with her missionary parents in Colombia. She spoke fluent Spanish and was active in the church's outreach programs to the neighborhood's growing Hispanic community. Her husband, Rudy, was quiet, gentle, and scholarly. With Rudy and Sara, I discussed and bemoaned US involvement in El Salvador and the attempts to undermine the Nicaraguan Sandinista government. Michael and I drove with them and their two children, Joel and Laura, to view the spectacular New England fall foliage, and when I went into the hospital for minor surgery, Michael stayed with Sara and Rudy, as he did when I traveled to do a reading at a college. If Rudy and Sara needed to get away for the weekend, Laura and Joel stayed with Michael and me. For the last three years I lived in Boston, this network of friends and friendships became the surrogate family that I had known my son and I needed, that we could not in fact have lived successfully without.

I fashioned a multicultural, interracial world for Michael to be cared for and sheltered by. This church family worked in tandem with my actual family and friends, made up of people like an old friend of my mother's whom I had always called "Aunt" Bert. Thelbert Hines had come to Washington, DC, from Wilson, North Carolina, in the same era during which my mother left Greensboro. She at one time had managed one of my mother's rooming houses and had witnessed her marriage to and separation from my father. She celebrated my mother's gambling wins with her, helped her grieve over financial and emotional losses. When my mother died, I asked Aunt Bert if I could consider her my surrogate mother, and she said, "Of course, dear, you know you can." I did not need, however, to ask her to be grandmother to Michael. Each Valentine's Day, a birthday card arrived in the mail for my son with a money gift inside. Christmas gifts she allowed Michael to choose, visiting us and turning a shopping trip into a family reunion. But most important, Aunt Bert called regularly, frequently. She did not require a season or a holiday to drop us a line or give us a call to make sure we were okay. This woman represented the spirit of extended family and extended love that had enabled Blacks to survive, 'buked and scorned but with pride.

• • •

My task as a Black parent was to enable my son to positively assert and define himself in a society that had perfected diminishment of who and what he really was. But the group morality of my community and the external realities imposed upon us required that Michael become culturally flexible and open. I wanted him to meet whites and Hispanics and Asians and people of all races whom he could befriend and respect, to give him a sense of the breadth of human possibility. I also wanted him to recognize early on that whether or not he was "equal" to anyone else was a question that was offensive, superfluous, and irrelevant.

Watching Rudy read stories to Laura and Joel or talk with Sara, Michael witnessed a family different from the one he and I comprised. He saw that "family" often defied singular definition. And I watched my son, content and secure in the expanded domestic realm we—strangers, friends, parents—had created. Michael simply liked and trusted the Maxwell clan. With my own family miles away in other cities, they served as an immediate, present source of support for us both. The intense mutual dependence of mother and child in one-parent homes can breed in children anxiety and fear, often unexpressed, about the safety, future, and health of the parent. If I worried about what would happen to Michael if I died, I know that he was haunted as well by the same fear.

The Maxwells allowed Michael to claim a larger, more resilient sense of what he was connected to, what he could count on, and who would be there for him when I could not be. I measured Michael's satisfaction in the ease with which he climbed on Rudy's lap for a story, and in the manner in which Laura and Joel made room for Michael in the circle of their father's affection. I saw it manifested in the generosity with which my son shared our home with his young friends. I became friends as well with Janiece, a Black woman who was a member of our "small group." She was divorced, and her former husband often took Michael along on Saturday outings with him and their son, Jason. I knew I was lucky, as well as blessed, in the wondrous magnanimity with which we as parents salvaged and inspired the best that we possessed for the sake of our children.

In our friendship, Sara and I were spiritual and emotional confidantes. She had been married for a decade and had been a full-time wife and mother. She admired my career and my various journeys. I was attracted to her deep religious faith and her generosity, which led her to work in the church co-op and engage in numerous community projects that cared for the elderly, the illiterate, and the poor. Sara possessed a political savvy that most people thought was simply charm but that constantly intrigued me as I watched it unfold, whether in her handling of church matters or in dealing with social service agencies for a newly arrived immigrant.

One afternoon as we sat in her apartment sipping tea, Sara observed suddenly, "You know, I really admire how well you handle being a single parent."

"How well?" I asked, genuinely surprised.

"Yes, I mean I just don't know if I could do it, if something happened to Rudy," she said, hugging a throw pillow as she sat on the sofa, as if to shield herself from the implications of the thought.

"You'd do it if you had to."

"Yes, I guess you're right, but I just don't think I'd do it as well as you."

Reflexively, I wondered if Sara thought that as a Black woman, I was more prepared genetically, sociologically perhaps, to raise a child alone than she. I had no secret weapon, no special strengths as I raised Michael, acting as mother/father/breadwinner. And the support that she and Rudy provided had plugged up the holes in my steadfast but often vulnerable resolve. Yet in Sara's words I heard the pernicious "other side" of the mythology that hounded Black single mothers, a belief rooted in the stubborn remnants of the matriarchal myth.

Was this a genuine compliment, I wondered, one I was too insecure to accept gracefully, or did Sara harbor racial stereotypes that can cling even to a consciousness as independent and inclusive as hers? She was resilient, confident. I had witnessed her chair board meetings at church and rock Joel to sleep at night. Why would she question her ability to raise her children without a husband in the house? For the same reasons I wrestled with that question every day.

My insecurities were constantly fed and stoked by the larger society as well as my own community. Citing prisons filled to bursting with Black men, the exploding rates of homicide and teenage pregnancy, Blacks employing the time-honored tactic of female scapegoating argued that I could not accomplish this task. Conversely, whites felt that my history, my inherent psychological makeup, prepared me eminently, virtually by right, to shoulder this weight—and even more—alone. Was I incompetent or Amazon? I knew the answer, but its complexity discouraged anyone from hearing it, even when I gathered the courage to speak its name.

Remembering those years, I am awed by my hunger to have—by the determination I marshaled to invent—a family and a community for my son. When I think of the Black youth in crisis in our community, endangered by racism, incompetent parents, and dangerous home environments, I often have fantasies of forming a brigade of concerned men and women. We would simply walk into homes where our children were at risk, claim them in the name of the future, bundle them up, and take them into the many homes we have where love flourishes and order exists. In this vision, we are knocking on doors and defeating ignorance, hostility, even threats of violence, with the power of love for our children. Our righteous presence silences verbal threats, forces guns to slide from palms, empty their cartridges, and then disintegrate. We are on time. We are taking care of business. We are not waiting for things to get worse. We are loving our children and their lives completely, right now.

• • •

In the fall of 1983, I quit my job at Emerson College. I was in the grip of a depression, manifested by a severe case of teacher burnout. After eight years in the academy, in the past year I had found myself fleeing the eager faces of my students at the end of each class. Many mornings I overslept, preferring to stay in bed rather than take on another day. Many afternoons I walked down Tremont Street toward the Piano Factory choking on a backlog of barely suppressed tears. I yearned for some grand, shattering experience that would shake up the predictability of my life. My always fragile tolerance for Boston's tribalistic racial atmosphere was demolished when a Black man was run over by a subway train after being chased by a bat-wielding group of white men attempting to drive him out of their neighborhood, one of a series of brutal attacks by whites against Blacks that year which resulted in the death or maiming of the victim. I wanted Michael to grow up in a city where he could see Blacks in positions of power and authority. Even pseudo power (the only kind we really had) was better, I reasoned, than what he witnessed in Boston. The city had become an intolerable place for me as a Black woman to raise my son.

It was this desire to challenge and test myself, this willingness to delve into the unknown, this penchant for creating myself over and over again, that had given the life I lived with Michael its energy, drama, and wealth. When we traveled from city to city and country to country, we were pilgrims. Each time we packed our bags, I was informing my son that the world was his. And so, I quit a good job, moved out of a spacious brick-walled, hardwood-floored apartment, and said goodbye to our surrogate family and a host of friends—this time, to go home.

Since leaving Washington after graduating from college, I had avoided even the thought of returning there to live. For me, the city was possessed by the ghosts of the mother and father who had not just died but had, I felt, deserted me. But Washington was politically and racially more hospitable than Boston, I had relatives there, and while I would have to start over again, by this point in my life, that thought no longer frightened me, and some days I wondered if it ever really had.

A year after my return "home," I met Philip, a photographer and graphic artist. Moody, aesthetic, he told me once he had considered becoming a priest. He, too, had traveled and lived in Africa, and like me, he was searching for union with a spirit and a soul that echoed his own. Six months after we met, we began living together. We talked of marriage but never went through with it. His mother had died of cancer when he was ten. Sometimes, memories of his childhood in the projects on welfare, of being shuttled during his mother's illness and after her death between the homes of relatives who considered him a burden, of not knowing who his father was, overwhelmed him and he burrowed within himself, silent and withdrawn for days at a time.

Yet in his relationship with Michael, Philip consistently found a way to tunnel a path out of his own private darkness. He, who had never known his own father, became a loving and loved, discipline-demanding, communicative, nurturing father figure to Michael. Philip taught my son karate, spent hours on Saturday afternoons with him in the video arcade, watched Sunday afternoon Redskins games with him, supervised his homework, and by his presence provided my son with a living model of maleness to imitate and respect. And Philip taught me, for Michael's sake, to loosen my maternal grip on the son I loved more than my own life.

In our relationship, however, Philip was less assured, and our affair was as tumultuous as his relationship with Michael was steady. We both desperately wanted to forge ties that would bind. But in the end, Philip possessed too many demons he could not overcome. His insecurities fed and stoked mine. I often felt imprisoned by a cauldron of feelings that were passionate, extreme, mercurial. Mostly, loving Philip, I felt out of control.

Sometime after the first year of our affair, I knew it had to end. But Philip's talent with Michael, his absolute loyalty to and concern for my son, always gave me pause. Maybe, just maybe, we can make this work, I told myself over and over, the words sounding more hollow, more false each time. I repeated them like a weary mantra. Since I was a parent, my life unfolded before my son's eyes on an invisible stage. Every day he had a front-row seat. Soon I was willing to admit that whatever confidence Philip instilled in my son through his affection for him was undercut by the conflicts Michael witnessed between Philip and me.

How well did he really love my son, I wondered, if he loved me so ineptly? How would Michael learn to be open with a woman as he watched me unsuccessfully chip away at the boulder of silence that Philip, like Femi, too often imposed? I shuddered at the thought that in my relationship with Philip, I was informing Michael that love was some restless, quake-and-thunder-filled landscape, that I was teaching him the lesson I had learned from my parents: that real love hurts, a lesson it took me twenty years to defeat and deny.

I spent nearly nine months deciding what to do, a period of backsliding, second-guessing my most trusted instincts, and being racked with guilt about the impact of my decision (whichever one I chose) on Michael. Then one day, two years after Philip moved in, I woke up one morning and, by noon, told him he had to leave. He vigorously resisted my request, countering my assertion that whatever we once had was over with promises I had heard before. But I was not in the throes of a "mood," as he chose to believe, one I could be cajoled or talked out of. I wanted my life back. I was ready to live without Philip, realized, in fact, that if peace was to inhabit the home I was making for my son, Philip would have to leave.

I chose, as I had when I left Femi, to place my emotional health and the needs of my son on an equal footing. My decision was not simply a matter of putting me first. I was raised by a mother who walked away from three husbands when the love they offered degenerated into the confining or the destructive. And so I knew that in leaving Philip, I would, once I got past the pain, find an equilibrium, a confidence that my son needed in his mother much more than he required a "man in the house." I would hurt. Michael would too. But I could hold on to him, urge him to hold on to me and cling to the strengths that resided within himself, as we stumbled through it all.

• • •

I heard the laughter of the neighborhood children playing outside, heard a bat thunder against a ball, hoping, as I wrote another line, that no windows were broken. And I sat listening, as I often did, for Michael's voice. I had written five pages nonstop, and tossing the pen aside to rest my aching fingers, I looked up and saw my son standing in the doorway of my bedroom.

At eleven, he was tall. That evening, however, he stood with his shoulders hunched in despair and brooding defeat. The lips that smiled so easily and so often were pursed, a grim, unforgiving line etched across his face. His eyes were so vacant, there was no way to even guess what thoughts plagued him at that moment. The effect Philip's departure had on Michael introduced me to a side of my son I had simply never seen before.

The reasoned explanations for my breakup with Philip, which I had practiced and then delivered like a transparent political speech, had only increased Michael's grief and anger. Philip was the only father figure my son had ever known intimately. And the day Michael came home from school to find all of Philip's clothes removed from the closets and his photos stripped from the walls, my son locked the door to his room and refused to come out until the next morning.

A few days later when Michael was running late for school, I entered his room and found him standing before his chest of drawers gripping the top of the bureau, his teeth clenched, his eyes red from crying. I touched his shoulder and he flinched, turning to look at me, his look slicing me into tiny pieces. When I asked what was wrong, he whispered, "I feel so angry. I'm so mad. I want to kill somebody."

I held him, hugged him close, but he refused to cry in my arms and I felt him against me brittle, sealed shut.

That spring evening, however, several months after Philip had left, I braved a tiny smile, patted a spot on the bed beside me, and asked, "What's wrong?"

Dropping his catcher's mitt on the floor, Michael sat on the bed beside me.

"Nothing," he said, shrugging.

"Nothing? I don't believe that."

Michael sat picking his fingernails, dirt-filled from play, hedging, gathering courage. Frightened by the depth of Michael's grief over Philip's departure, unable alone to help him sort through and master his conflicted emotions, I had arranged for him to see a counselor at Howard University, Audrey Chapman, a family therapist. She had told me how difficult it would be for Michael to reveal his pain. As I was the only parent he had, he feared that if he angered me, he might lose everything. But sitting beside my son at that moment, I did not feel like the omnipotent controller of his life that to his young eyes and in his young mind I was. I sat beside him feeling, as I imagined he felt then, small, tremulous, and afraid.

"What's that?" he asked, pointing to a diary I had been writing in.

"A journal I'm keeping."

"About what?"

"About you and me."

"And Philip?"

"And Philip."

"Who is my family besides you?" he asked finally, slowly, carefully, after poking at the beginnings of a hole in his jeans and staring at his hands and daring a quick look at me from the corner of his eyes, a look that retreated so fast, maybe I didn't see it at all.

"What do you mean? You know who your family is."

"All the other kids have cousins and stuff. Edward told me he's going to a family reunion next week. Where's my family?" he asked angrily, now looking at me head-on.

"You want cousins?" I asked, thinking fast. "I've got cousins in North Carolina and they've got kids, so that means you've got cousins too."

"How come we never see them?"

"We're just not that close."

"How come?"

"No reason. We just aren't."

"How will I ever see them?"

"Well, I'll call them, I'll let them know that we want to visit them."

"When?"

"Soon."

I had mastered the art of burning bridges. Now my son was demand-ing that I build some instead, and lead him across them into the arms of people at whom he could look and see a facial feature, watch a walk, hear a laugh that he would recognize because blood made it his too. That evening I heard what my son had asked. I heard what he did not say. Michael had chosen to ask me for his father by asking for his family. Two or three times a year I had practiced a ritual with my son. We would spend an evening going through photos of his father, pictures that captured the woman I had been, the life I had lived in Nigeria. My son knew who his father was, and I told him again and again rationally, precisely, that his father was a good man who loved him and whom I had loved, but that because of problems I could not solve, I had had to leave him.

Children possess an emotional radar their parents never suspect. Michael had to have sensed the tenseness, the stilted quality that invaded my voice when I spoke of his father and that belied the intent of every word. And when he asked, as he sometimes did, when he would see his father and I answered too quickly, brusquely at times, "One day," I know now how impossible and even cruel that must have sounded to his young ears. For I loomed like a genie over the landscape of his life, in full possession of the power, he thought, to easily retrieve his father if I wanted to. He could not imagine my fear of losing him, the fear I felt as I imagined opening our lives up to Femi once again.

I had used my fear for Michael's safety to justify denying Femi access to his son. But wasn't my arbitrary separation of father and son as cruel as Femi's threats to take Michael from me? Fear had inspired me to interrupt and possibly stall the dynamic of healing that might have arrived sooner than I thought. I dreaded seeing Femi as much because of the guilt I felt as because I imagined recrimination and anger as his only possible responses to me. In my anguished fantasies, I never once assumed that Femi would be capable of rejoicing in reunion with his son rather than castigating me.

Audrey Chapman told me of the sessions where Michael talked about Philip, how much he missed him, how angry he was at me for making him leave. She told me that finally in the third session, Michael had cried, wept long and hard for the father figure he had lost and the father he did not know. For Philip's love, his presence in our life, and his leaving had become a catalyst that disturbed the dormant wound of my son's absent, unknown father. Some sessions, she asked Michael to draw pictures of Nigeria and his father, and he used the crayons and pencils to shape tentative yet hopeful sketches that they discussed and analyzed. But Michael never once mentioned them to me.

Near the end of Michael's sessions with Chapman, she told me that some issues had surfaced in their conversations which she thought I should be aware of. And, she said, she felt that Michael should tell me face-to-face what these "issues" were. "Children are deeply affected by the decisions their parents make," she said, trying to calm the apprehension she saw clearly in the worried expression on my face. "Yet rarely are they permitted to honestly and openly tell parents how they feel, how they've been affected by those choices." I loved my son, but even for me, a parent who had forged often unconventional answers to the challenges we faced, the prospect of submitting to an assessment of my life rendered by Michael terrified me.

The day of the joint session arrived, after an anxious week of waiting and wondering what Michael was going to say. Chapman began the session by talking for several minutes about the importance of what was going to take place and the significance of Michael's feelings. Then Michael, without an instant of hesitation (although I had expected a few moments' reprieve), turned and asked, "Mom, why'd you stay with Philip all that time?" I felt myself crumbling beneath his patient gaze and the confusion I heard in his voice.

"Well," I began slowly, stalling for time, "I loved him." I sat wondering how bad this was going to get. Yet even as I told him this, the words "I loved him" sounded like a hurriedly conceived excuse for a major crime.

"But he made you feel bad. I could tell."

"He wasn't a very happy person," I said lamely, the muddy tapestry of my relationship with Philip slowly rising before my mind's eye.

"But he made you feel unhappy." So, I hadn't been able to hide anything, I thought, amazed at and grateful for the level of my son's empathy.

"I wanted him to stay because I knew he cared for you. You cared for him." At twelve, without the guidance of a counselor schooled in psychology, I had asked my mother the same questions about my father. I had found it unfathomable that she could not simply walk away from a man who so often made her miserable. When she told me she remained with my father in part because of his love for me, the conflicts and contradictions of the answer, its heartfelt and heartbreaking demands, were more than my adolescent mind could comprehend. Now I was a woman who had walked in my mother's shoes. I knew some part of what my son felt at that moment.

"Yeah, I liked him a lot. It's just that it made me feel sad when he made you get upset or angry."

"Why didn't you say something?"

Michael gazed at Audrey Chapman, then told me, "I wanted to help, to make you feel better. Mom, I didn't know how."

The scheduled forty-five minutes turned into an hour and a half as Michael confessed that his loyalty to me had competed with what he felt for Philip. He had wanted Philip to stay. But seeing my misery, he wanted him to leave. And his inability to intervene in the skirmishes that flared between Philip and me increased his sense of helplessness and his lack of faith in us both.

How do I assess what my son lost in those years without his father? How dare I? Femi's need to control by instilling fear, my repudiation of the past through possession of our son, had left us all bereft, stripped of vital connections. I hail myself as a writer, yet even with words I am afraid to attempt a precise computation of the toll. In the end, I know only that I was a mother who loved her child. In the end, I did not make the "right" choice as much as I made the choice I could live with.

And yet, along the way, my son came to his own conclusions. One evening we sat reading together. I frequently chose to explore a book with Michael, with each of us alternately reading passages and discussing the text. He was twelve then, and we were reading the autobiography of the athlete Bo Jackson. In the book, Bo spoke candidly of growing up poor and of the anger he had often felt and directed at his mother. Bo recounted numerous incidents of youthful antisocial behavior, spawned, he felt, by his resentment of his absent father and his mother's inability to provide adequately for her children. But it was clear that what angered Bo most was the precariousness, the meagerness of his life, the constant material need. His anger was so forcefully stated that I paused in my reading to ask Michael if in growing up with only one parent, he had ever felt similar emotions.

His answer was astonishingly quick and confident. "No," he told me with a vehement shake of his head. "You've done everything a man could do." My son was judging my effectiveness as a parent. He was also disputing the myth that love alone is enough. Children need to see their parents as capable of providing for them. Watching parents do this, children learn that the world is a fair and reasonable sphere for them to enter, one that they can trust.

• • •

As I had promised Michael, I contacted my cousins, and, several months later, we journeyed to Greensboro for a wonderful reunion. And a week after the talk in my bedroom, I wrote his father. I had decided to write Femi once Audrey Chapman revealed to me what was coming out in the sessions with her. But it required several weeks of prayer, meditation, and rejecting the advice of friends who cautioned, "You've ensured your son's safety all these years, why risk it now?" before I sat down one evening and wrote a two-paragraph letter to my former husband.

I was exhausted by the years of fear. And I was more afraid of my son never forgiving me if I denied him his father than of any attempt his father might make to take him from me. I was a risk taker. And I computed with my heart and my head that Michael and I had nothing to lose and everything to gain by reaching out to his father now.

In this I was following the script my mother had written for me. Despite my father's numerous affairs and the ruthless manner in which he squandered her financial resources, my mother insisted that I respect and love my father. "He's the only father you've got," she'd tell me. "And that means you have to love him." Whatever bitterness she felt, she refused to pass it on to me. Because I grew up loving "the only father I had," it was imperative that I give my son his father too.

Six weeks after I wrote Femi, I received a response. The envelope contained a letter for me and one for Michael. The tone of the letter was grateful, conciliatory, and without a trace of the recrimination I had feared. I raced upstairs with the letter when I pulled it from the mailbox, shouting for Michael as I entered the apartment. I had told him I had written his father but had been careful to caution him that I could not predict when we would hear from him, or even if he would write back. My son and I sat that afternoon reading first his letter, then the one Femi had sent to me, over and over. Michael was smiling for the first time in months as he held his letter. After a while he took it into his room and lay on his bed reading it and holding it, and then placed it beside his plate at dinner.

In the months that followed, Femi and I wrote frequently. I sent him photos of Michael. He sent us pictures of himself. The morning we made our first call to Lagos to speak with Femi, I woke Michael up at five in the morning (because of the time difference) to speak with his father in his office. The first call was stilted, a bit awkward for us all. Michael sat on the edge of his bed, drowsy, his eyes filled with sleep, yet smiling and satisfied as his father plied him with questions about school, his friends, his hobbies, and his ambitions. And soon Femi's brother Bade, who lived in Brooklyn, became Femi's stand-in, calling frequently, updating Michael and me on news of the family in Nigeria.

Six months after I received Femi's letter, Michael and I spent a weekend with my cousin Debra and her husband and young son in Edison, New Jersey. My cousin was a vice president at one of the largest banks in New York City. She had enthusiastically supported the idea of my contacting Femi. A year before I left Nigeria, Debra had visited me. She liked and respected Femi, yet was part of a small but important circle of support I had relied on during the days and months when I first returned to the United States. We had a long talk that weekend about Michael spending more time with her family so that her husband Ed could take him fishing on his boat and play a more pronounced "big uncle" role. Debra's relationship with her father, my mother's brother, had been sometimes distant and sporadic in the years before his death, yet her memories of him were generous and affectionate. And so Debra knew how much Michael needed a "congregation" of fathers, formal and informal, to surround him.

Sunday morning of that weekend, Michael and I took the train from my cousin's house into New York and met Bade at Penn Station. Femi's father was polygamous, and Bade and Femi were not born of the same mother. Yet they were bound by the blood of their father and so their brotherhood was considered complete. Always the family mediator, Bade was a gentle man whose warmth had made him one of my favorite Ajayis when we first met in Nigeria.

Bade was accompanied by his wife, Cecilia, and their three children. For Bade, my son was Akintunde, not Michael, and he embraced him, assuring him that even during the years of estrangement, he had never been forgotten. Cecilia and I chatted on the subway to Brooklyn, and Bade plied Michael with questions and then sat silent for long moments, holding Michael's hand, marveling at the sight of him. In Bade's apartment, Michael gave his young cousins Akin, Lola, and Fola the video games I had brought for them and helped them improve their Nintendo skills. After a traditional dinner of chicken and jollof rice, Bade showed Michael a large black-and-white photo of his great-great-great-grandfather. In the photo, the man was draped in royal robes and sat flanked by several courtiers. Bade told Michael a story of service by their royal ancestor to a king, of Ajayi bravery in war, fidelity in marriage, of Ajayi children born generation after generation, of Ajayi migrations from the midsection of the country to the western coast. Michael sat rapt, quiet, blessed. And then Bade gave Michael a picture of Femi's father dressed in formal robes and speaking into a microphone, obviously addressing a crowd. He was tall, imposing, with the face of a leader, which, as a chief and owner of hundreds of acres of land, he was in his community.

Then there was a call to Nigeria so that Michael could speak with Bade's sister. Bade reached his sister Folake, who used to be a seamstress in their hometown of Ado Ekiti but who now was a contractor selling everything from cement to foodstuffs. She and I talked, her greeting to me ecstatic, studded with short prayers thanking God that she was hearing my voice. Then she spoke with Michael. It did not matter that my son had no memory of this woman who knew him three days after his birth. What mattered was that he, like she, was an Ajayi, and her lavish, enthusiastic greeting had been saved for this moment. That Sunday the meaning of my son's name, "the spirit of the father returns," was never more true. Bade walked us to the subway that evening, and we promised to stay in touch, a promise we both kept.

On the train back to Washington, Michael was quiet and reflective, and at one point asked, "If my great-great-great-grandfather was a king, what does that make me?" I could feel how energized and satisfied he was by this day. "I guess that makes you a prince," I said, smiling, and squeezed his hand.

• • •

Back in Washington, as Michael moved closer to adolescence, I fashioned a bulwark of concerned adults to surround and help guide him. I applied for a Big Brother for him, and he was partnered with a young Black investment banker named Loren Tate. Loren not only took Michael to the requisite baseball and basketball games but took him to his job one day to spend a few hours watching him work; and even when the demands of his work did not allow him to see Michael as often as he preferred, he made up for that with telephone conversations. Watching Loren with my son, I learned as I had with Philip that while fathers may not be required in the lives of young boys, capable, caring men are. And I knew, too, that all the "male role models" in the world could not reach a boy unless he had been consistently, purposely loved and cared for, unless he had already been taught and was prepared to trust himself and others.

Missing the emotional support that Philip had offered, I formed a single parents' group. I put the word out through friends and placed an ad in the city paper, and soon there were seven of us, six women and one man, meeting once a month. We were divorced parents as well as never married: teachers, librarians, accountants. For the next two years, what we did was both simple and monumental. We met at each other's homes one Saturday afternoon each month.

While our kids, who ranged in age from three to sixteen, played in the basement, watched movies, or shot baskets outside, we sat in the kitchen and talked. We were all hardy survivors of the love-and-marriage wars, and we talked about our kids and our fears for them, shared what had worked with them and what had not. We went on picnics and to the beach in the summer, took the kids to the roller rink. Aaron acted as a big brother to the boys, taking them to wrestling matches and basketball games. The rest of us were occasional big sisters to Aaron's two daughters. We shared news of jobs, raises, broken hearts; we babysat for each other. Mostly what we did was consistently provide an understanding, listening ear, one hooked in instinctively to the special needs our status as single parents imposed.

The most perplexing blemish on the surface of those years was my son's inconsistent, often lackluster, performance in school. He never failed a grade, but year after year I was called to his school by teachers who complained of his disorganization and sloppiness, his playing in class and poor attention span. My son was the product of a culturally "overrich" home, yet his often average-to-mediocre performance baffled me as well as his teachers, who told me repeatedly, "He's the brightest kid in the class when he applies himself. But so often his work doesn't reflect the level he could attain."

Though Michael was clearly exuberant and highly sociable, he was not hyperactive, which would have sent me to a doctor for a diagnosis of his behavior. I was confused because at home, I watched Michael build model airplanes, read, write raps, and follow the intricate instructions of TV cooking shows with undiminished and laser-like concentration. What happened to that focus and that intensity at school? Like Michael's teachers, I simply assumed that my son was merely immature and would soon "buckle down," particularly since punishments and a strictly imposed study schedule at home seemed to have little influence on improving performance at school.

• • •

I met Joe Murray at a party given by one of the members of the single-parents group. He was a forty-three-year-old high school teacher of math and computers who arrived at the party with two longtime male friends, Issa N'dour, a Senegalese with whom he had traveled to Mexico, and Lawrence Berry, a fellow teacher. Throughout the evening, he joked and parried with these men in a way that revealed the depth of their friendship. And he approached me with no rap, no line, wearing his maleness easily, with nothing to prove. On the dance floor, he informed me that he was supposed to be in the Dominican Republic but that the host, Tina, his old friend and "play sister" who taught with him at Dunbar High School, had threatened never to speak to him again if he didn't cancel his trip and come to the party. Joe talked with me and Louise, my closest friend, who was refreshing. Though he was clearly interested, I never felt as though I was being "hit on" or assessed.

On our first date, over dinner in a Black-owned restaurant, Joe said, "I wish you'd had a chance to meet my daughter before she left for California." In those words I heard a declaration of the fierce loyalty he felt toward his family. He was the father as well of a two-year-old son whom he saw once a week. When I asked why he had never married, he told me, "I refused to get married just because other people or society thought it was time or if I thought it wouldn't last." After dinner, we drove to a street near Capitol Hill where he had just purchased a house that he planned to renovate and turn into a rental property. He told me that evening about his five trips to Brazil, a visit to Suriname, the pen pals he had all over the world. He was the kind of kid, he said, who, when he played cowboys and

Indians, had volunteered to be an Indian because his parents had told him about the West from the Indians' point of view. Joe's family was close-knit, politically active in DC politics, and respected. They welcomed Michael and me into their midst as though our presence enhanced who they were.

Within a few weeks, I was beginning to love the way Joe combined a sense of adventure and a quirky skepticism in the face of conventional wisdom with a healthy respect for the practical and the secure. One Saturday afternoon, Joe spent several hours with Michael and me eating crabs, watching movies on video, and talking. He did not charge into the space I had created with my son as though it was his to remake simply because he was a man. Joe Murray won over Michael not by trying to be "Daddy" but by being himself. On Sunday, Joe often brought his son, Austin, to my house, where he played with Michael. Early in their relationship, Michael made Austin two three-foot-tall baseball players out of cardboard, painted their uniforms, and drew their features in so lifelike a manner that Austin wondered if they were real. For months, whenever he came to my house, the first thing Austin asked for was "baseball man."

• • •

Just as Joe and I became lovers, as I savored my son's reconciliation with his father, just as the pieces finally seemed at last to fit, my son careened into adolescence. I heard the deepening of Michael's voice, witnessed the growth spurts that propelled him to a height that echoed his father's, saw the sudden appearance of muscles—and a bikini-clad Jet centerfold plastered on his bedroom wall. I was flushed with trepidation. Soon Michael would inhabit that narrow, corrupt crawl space in the minds of whites and some Black people too, a space reserved for criminals, outcasts, misfits, and Black men. Soon he would become a permanent suspect.

Saving Our Sons

Seeing him, women would think twice about entering elevators alone with him, cops would slow down in their patrol cars, watch him a little more closely when he walked down the street. Store owners would automatically assign the security guard to keep an eye on him when he entered the door. And there was nothing I could do. By the time my son was twelve, every day I wondered when he left me in the morning what would be the manner of his return to me at night.

This move by Michael into a new stage of his life made me realize more than ever how important it was to choose a boyfriend or husband who would bring his own special talents into our family circle. My son missed nothing. He witnessed my love affairs and was influenced by them. Any man who entered our life influenced my son explicitly and implicitly, providing cues and lessons and models for adulthood and manhood. After the breakup with Philip, I assessed the men I dated more carefully. It became important to know what their attitudes were toward their own family, if they had friendships with both sexes—or friendships with anyone, if they were satisfied with their work, if they were men who sought to creatively control their fate rather than sink into bitterness or complaint about what they had not achieved, if they cheered me on in my own work, if in their relationship with me they were seeking an equal partner or only a helpmate, if they felt secure enough in themselves to accept the depth of the bond Michael and I shared. One day my son would fall in love, and I wanted to teach him lessons about love that he would not have to discard or question because he found them tripping him up or ensnaring him. My love, I now knew, was also my son's legacy of love.

Joe and I discussed marriage six weeks after we met but decided to wait a year before making a final decision. Neither Joe nor Michael felt the need to compete for my affection or attention. Until Michael turned fourteen, when suddenly all adults became intolerable, his relationship with Joe was relatively tension-free. As the months passed and it became clear that Joe and I would indeed marry, I wanted Michael to tell me what he thought of the changes such a move would introduce into our lives.

"What do you think of Joe?" I asked him over dinner.

"He's an all right dude." More and more with each passing year, the youngster who despite average grades had scored two grades above his level on standardized tests resorted to vague generalities, shrugs, and grunts, even groans, to express himself.

"Okay, you've got to translate for me. Just what does that mean?" I asked, giving Michael my I-mean-business look as he reached for a glass of water.

"He's okay."

"Only okay?"

"You know what I mean," he said, shrugging for the third time.

"No, I don't. Tell me what you like about him."

"Aw, Mom, do I have to?" he moaned, as though I had asked him to endure the Chinese water torture.

"Yes, you do."

"Why?"

"Because we're getting married."

"I knew that," he said, unimpressed.

"You did?"

"Sure."

"How?"

"I could tell."

"How?"

"I just could. I'm only thirteen, but I'm not stupid."

"That means he'll be your stepfather. And you'll have a sister in Keesha and a brother in Austin."

"Uh-huh." He had dived back into the food on his plate.

"Can you handle that?"

"Sure," he said, giving me an are-you-kidding stare.

"You can?"

"Sure. Joe's a decent guy. I mean, like, he works all those jobs. He's got two houses. He's done stuff." I could hear the respect that Michael would never openly admit.

"So you think he'll be able to take care of us?"

"Sure."

"What are we going to give him?"

"What do you mean?"

"Well, we'll get this all right dude as a father and husband. And we'll get his kids and his family that already treats us like kin. What will we give him?"

"I don't know."

"You can't think of anything?"

"A perfect son and a beautiful wife."

"That's obvious." I laughed. "But what else?"

"I don't know." Another shrug.

"Our love. Our loyalty. Our respect."

"I knew that." He grinned smartly.

"You may not ever love Joe like a father, Michael, but if you give him half a chance, I know you can respect and honor him as somebody who cares about you. That's all I ask, okay?"

"Okay. Don't worry, Mom. I think you picked the right one this time."

TROUBLE THE WATERS

The decision made during the fall of Michael's ninth-grade year to send him to a private boarding school was born of years of frustration in the face of lackluster, indifferent grades from an obviously bright and talented child. I had taken him out of the public schools once before when he was a fifth grader, and enrolled him in an excellent private academy whose curriculum was Afrocentric-based. But even there, with smaller classes and more one-on-one attention from the teachers, Michael still performed with less success than intelligence and other standardized tests indicated he could. As the prospect of high school neared, I felt a radical step had to be taken. Greater structure, a more rigorous curriculum, and a setting where there was no reward from classmates for disruptive behavior had turned around the sons of friends. I hoped that such a change would get Michael on the right track too. In addition, a boarding school began to seem an attractive alternative as the violence in the schools increased.

• • •

In early January of 1993, I decided to keep a diary. This would be the year that Michael would see his father and that he would possibly go away to school. I wanted to freeze and permanently possess the events and emotions that would define that year in my son's life. I kept a diary as well to meditate on and overcome the psychic toll imposed by the continuing murders of Black youth. Washington, DC, was becoming a killing field. A diary would provide me with a space where the blood did not flow, could not reach me, although its pages in time were consumed by my struggle to understand why death enthralled so many youngsters, why it seemed more seductive than life.

JANUARY 6, 1993

Went to the library today and looked through a guide to Independent Schools, trying to get a sense of options for Michael. I also called two of the schools Audrey Chapman's sister-in-law suggested and asked for catalogues. Susan Shreve told me about a Quaker school, Westtown, outside of Philadelphia. The headmaster there was formerly at Sidwell Friends. Susan says he took her son under his wing when he was going through a difficult time and helped him a lot.

I'm definitely going through with this, feel I have no other choice. My son is running out of time and chances. Michael's behavior in the fall term was inexcusable. We got a call from his science teacher reporting that he had loudly and for the raucous entertainment of the entire class mocked her Indian accent. The assistant principal called one afternoon to report that Michael had cursed at her, and as usual there were the requests from several teachers for conferences to discuss Michael's behavior and poor performance. Nothing seems to work—groundings, no television, no phone calls—nothing induces a change in behavior or performance. That's why a boarding school has begun to look attractive as a possibility. Michael is screaming for structure and a kind of discipline neither the public schools nor Joe and I can provide. But I still feel some discomfort in all this. I remember attending Columbia University for graduate school and the often primitive racism behind the school's elite ivy-covered walls.

I know that the stereotype of the prep school as a haven for spoiled rich kids from conservative homes is outdated, but what is the reality, and is it one that will fit my son? In bed last night, I lay for a long time beside Joe, curled into a fetal ball, missing Michael already, wondering if we could find a school that had enough Black kids so that he would feel comfortable. Last night Joe and I talked about where the money would come from to send Michael to a boarding school (the money somehow always comes). And we talked as well about interracial dating, or as I put it, "the white girl issue." My professional and personal life is interracial and often cross-cultural, but I still view my son as a resource for the race; with the distressing statistics Black women face when seeking a mate now and in the future, if I can produce a healthy, successful Black man, I want him to partner with a Black woman. We talked about all this and more, and yet still concluded that any girl Michael brought home would be judged on her character and not her skin color.

JANUARY 8, 1993

Sat down this evening and surveyed my finances, what's coming in and what's going out this year, and it appears that I can afford to take Michael to Nigeria this summer. Femi and I have talked often about a possible trip in our calls, and he has frequently mentioned this in his letters. For a variety of reasons, I feel this summer is the right time. I think this first trip, two weeks is long enough. No way can we make up for all the years lost even if Michael stayed a month. But at least this year I'll do what has been long overdue.

JANUARY 10, 1993

The brochure, video, and application form from Westtown arrived in the mail today. The video is instructive and entertaining, but it's hard to know how much is reality and how much is PR. The financial aid form is a book in itself, is terribly intrusive, and asks for more data than the Internal Revenue Service. I doubt we'll qualify for aid, but I want to give it a shot anyway. Michael, still sulking over the prospect of attending boarding school, refused to look at the Westtown video this evening.

JANUARY 18, 1993

This morning I called Nigeria and spoke with Femi, told him about Michael's behavior in school, which earned Michael a 6 a.m. transatlantic lecture from his father. We talked about my plans to visit him this summer with Michael.

JANUARY 19, 1993

Went to B. Dalton today and bought several books for Michael to read, including **Bloods** *by Wallace Terry,* **Black Boy** *by Richard Wright,* **The Chocolate War** *by Robert Cormier,* **Tiger Eyes** *by Judy Blume. He may be a slacker at school, but I refuse to let him slack off at home. I plan to give him two weeks to read each book and then give him an essay test on each one.*

JANUARY 21, 1993

Michael's campaign to dissuade me on the boarding school issue continues. Tonight it consisted of an attempt to discuss it with me "reasonably," with promises of better grades and behavior. When I told him it was too late, I was subjected to "The Look," a gaze of utter, total contempt that involves a tight muscular pursing of the lips, a trenchant rolling and simultaneous narrowing of the eyes. Part of The Look also involves a steeling of the body and a quick, dismissive turning away from the subject that presents the back full-fledged, embellished by hunched, angry shoulders. I have had it with The Look and grabbed him by the collar—yes, at five feet two, I grabbed my five-foot-eight son by the collar of his T-shirt, yanked him up close into my face, and told him that I would slap The Look off his face the next time I saw it. We stood eye-to-eye, nose-to-nose, me staring up at him, him staring down at me. He was so furious, I could feel the anger on his skin, and in the midst of this, in the middle of the most horrid look on his face, I saw a tear roll down his cheek. I let him go then, for I felt such a cataclysmic mix of feelings, I started shouting at him to go to his room. And I didn't want him to possibly see me cry.

JANUARY 22, 1993

I talked with Jake for a while in his office at the Male Youth Program at Shiloh Baptist Church today. He explained the weight training program that he is designing for Michael. Then he told me that the staff took a poll of the boys in the program last week, asking what they feared most. The majority of the boys said, more than anything else, they feared being shot. Some of these kids routinely hear a symphony of gunfire riddling the air outside their homes at night. Former Mayor Marion Barry was in attendance at the program this afternoon with his son Christopher, who is enrolled. Barry, decked out in African-style clothing, looked good, clear-eyed and healthy. It is so hard to measure how the program is impacting Michael. But at least I know where he is after school, I know that he is supervised by caring capable adults and that his energies are being directed into positive outlets.

The Male Youth Program, begun by Shiloh in response to the increasing violence that ensnared so many young Black boys on the streets around the church, consists of an after-school study hall, supervised weight training, basketball, field trips, classes in computer literacy, and snacks and dinner. The program director, Jake Roach, is a veteran youth-development counselor who was a senior staff member of former Mayor Barry's Youth Leadership Initiative, one of the most successful programs of the Barry years. The outreach program trained the brightest young teens in the city in community service, academics, athletics, and leadership skills.

I asked Joyce Ladner once why the Black church had not done more in response to the crisis facing so many of our young people. Taking a deep breath and shaking her head, she told me, "You may *not believe this, but given the mentality, the deeply rooted conservatism of many of these churches, they've done as much as they can."*

"I don't accept that," I told her. "Look at how slow the church was in responding to the AIDS epidemic in our community, and as far as I'm concerned, they are still asleep on the issue of our youth, drug abuse, and crime."

"Remember," she continued, "the Black church is deeply rooted in the Protestant ethic and an essentially fundamentalist faith. The men and women who fill those churches on Sunday morning get up Monday through Friday and go to work, they pay their taxes, they obey the law. They fear God. And they simply cannot conceive of drug abuse, homosexuality, youth crime, teenaged pregnancy, and AIDS as resulting from anything other than a lapse in morals. They made it, they'll tell you, so why can't the young people. And they made it against odds that would make the younger generation tremble."

"But the church builds housing for the poor and elderly, sets up soup kitchens," I said.

"Yes, and the people affected by those services aren't carrying guns. Often the ministers and deacons are as afraid, as terrified, of the young boys on the street as we are. And so many of the young people now have virtually no connection to the church, whereas a generation ago somebody took you to church on Sunday so you were part of the community that the church created. All this makes it that much harder for these congregations to reach out to many of the people in our community most in need."

But at Shiloh, Reverend Henry Gregory had, a decade earlier, called together the men of the church after one Sunday morning service and with them had looked out his office window onto the grubby streets surrounding the church. Although the fashionable cars of the affluent congregation filled the streets that day, Reverend Gregory urged the deacons and others gathered to see instead the poverty and the violence that festered and grew inside the homes on many of the blocks adjacent to the building in which they stood. He charged them to build a way within Shiloh to save the young boys of the neighborhood. Noted sociologist Andrew Billingsley attended that meeting and told me, "When a Black Baptist minister gives you an assignment, believe me, it gets done."

Now at Shiloh, in the crowded basement space the program shares with a day-care center, Jake and his staff create an atmosphere where young boys feel safe. Jake regularly visits the schools attended by boys in the program to talk to teachers and counselors. He takes youths in potentially dangerous situations into his home while seeking social-service help for them. His staff of young male assistants is as dedicated and devoted as he is.

JANUARY 23, 1993

When Joe and I married, Michael and I moved into Joe's house on Eighth Street in Northwest Washington. The block is one of early-rising, hardworking middle-class Black professionals who battle dirt and crime with a combination of political savvy, righteousness, and community spirit. It is a street where neighbors have known each other long enough to report misbehaving youngsters to parents, who are grateful for the information, and where seniors, many of whom have lived on the block for decades, are accorded the status of respected elders. There is the requisite young white "homesteading" couple, who have renovated a house across the street from us. They of course are harbingers of the gentrification looming on the horizon. There are one or two families on welfare, but they are integrated into the life of the street as firmly as everyone else. Cleveland Elementary, one of the best schools in the city, known for its intense parental involvement, claims the corner adjacent to our house. And around the edges of Eighth Street, there is drug traffic.

JANUARY 25, 1993

This morning when Michael left for school, with Joe and I sitting in the car watching him walk down the street, we talked about Michael's adoption of the "gangster walk." He has begun to walk in the style that when we were young was called "pimping," a slightly cocked, rhythmic, almost three-quarter-beat mini-stagger young Black boys have long adopted for camouflage and protection. The walk says, "Don't f*** with me"; it asserts, "I'm cool"; and at its most hostile it says, "Beware." Shaking his head as he watched Michael walk toward the subway at the corner, Joe worried that he is simply overdoing the "cool pose." So intent on signaling that he is "cool" with his walk, Michael, Joe feels, is inadvertently signaling vulnerability, that rather than fitting into the neighborhood, he doesn't belong.

Joe worries that Michael will become a victim of his own unpolished bravado. I know that Michael lacks the steely inner core his gyrations imply he possesses. We both fear the consequences of a misreading of Michael's body language. If only these kids weren't armed to the teeth, if only they couldn't buy a gun as easily as a bag of potato chips, if only, if only, then we would worry less.

Since we moved onto the block, Michael has managed to navigate his way each day through the small knots of "drug boys" that claim the neighboring blocks, and he shoots ball and rides his bike with all the boys on the street. There are no hard-and-fast boundaries in the Black community. Even in the middle and upper classes, most of us are merely one generation away from poverty and one paycheck away from hard times if we lose our jobs. And so it is inevitable and even perhaps mandatory that Michael learn to say "What's happening" to the drug boys on Ninth Street and a polite "Hello" to Mr. Woods, our Neighborhood Advisory Council representative and the unofficial mayor of Eighth Street, when he passes by.

Saving Our Sons

JANUARY 26, 1993

The daily death toll recorded on the pages of the **Washington Post** *is controlled by a mysterious, primal, almost gothic aesthetic. The accounts of young Black males shot over a look, an imagined slight, turf, or a girl become a kind of literature, a never-ending, fascinating, horrible, unfolding saga. I yearn for the stories to end, yet find myself reading them obsessively in search of a new tale, a new death. Joe comes home from Dunbar in the afternoon with accounts of a handful of unruly, potentially lethal students who can create havoc all out of proportion to their numbers. The days when he could break up a fight are over, for now students are armed and could hurt him for not allowing them to settle a score. And because it gets dark by five, most evenings I drive three blocks to pick Michael up from Shiloh; I am that afraid for him.*

JANUARY 27, 1993

Have scheduled interviews for two private boarding schools, St. Andrews in Delaware and Westtown, for next month.

JANUARY 28, 1993

This evening we were gathered after dinner in the living room. Joe sat switching channels, and several images from Black Entertainment Television filled the screen, videos featuring, as they nearly always do, light-skinned, long-haired girls as the objects of affection, lust, and desire. The three of us span the color spectrum: Joe, light-skinned, what we used to call "redbone"; me, brown-skinned; Michael, caramel-colored. We have talked frankly, openly, about color in our house, about everything from why blondes are typecast as innocent/ dumb/good to why darker-skinned Black women most often play asexual roles and darker-skinned Black men criminals and heavies. Yet tonight, when Joe grimaced in disgust at the preponderance of light-skinned girls and the virtual absence of darker-skinned

---

beauties in the videos, Michael shouted, "You all always act like it's a conspiracy. It's no conspiracy that the girls look like that." We ended up arguing for fifteen minutes.

Later in the evening, when Joe turned to "For the People," a weekly show featuring interviews with Black historians, Michael laughed, "Everything was invented by the Black man, right? The Black man was the first one to invent the salt shaker!" Part of the program at Shiloh divides the boys into age groups, each named after Black men of note, and the boys get a heavy dose of Afrocentric education. This evening, Michael gloried in refuting everything Joe and I believe. Maybe we never really agreed. Maybe I took my son's silence as assent. Joe says he's just drunk on testosterone.

FEBRUARY 4, 1993

This evening, Michael and I went to Woodward & Lothrop to buy a suit for the visit to St. Andrews. Michael has decided now on a go-along-to-get-along tactic, abandoning his staunch, outspoken resistance to boarding school. I wonder what strategy he will spring on us next.

FEBRUARY 5, 1993

Michael came in from Shiloh this evening and headed straight upstairs into our bedroom, where for forty-five minutes he and Joe talked. When I asked Joe if there was a problem, he told me Michael had wanted to talk to him about something that had happened at school. Just before he went to bed, I cornered Michael in the kitchen and asked what was going on. It seems he is having a "problem" with a boy at school hassling him. He talked to Joe about what to do and how to handle the situation. When I asked why he didn't come to me, he shrugged and said, "You'd just get upset, but Joe, he knows what to tell me to do."

FEBRUARY 8, 1993

This morning, we drove up to Middletown, Delaware, for Michael's interview at St. Andrews. He was handsome in his first real suit—a double-breasted dark green jacket with a light yellow shirt and silk tie. During the two-hour drive, he finished **The Chocolate War.** *We talked about the moral dilemma the young hero faced and why he chose to handle it the way he did. We talked about what Michael would have done in the same situation. We also discussed the Judy Blume book, which I chose so he'd have to relate to a female protagonist. He said he liked Judy Blume's books because she "tells it like it is."*

We arrived forty-five minutes early, and after finding out where the administration building was, we ate lunch in a nearby diner. Michael said he was nervous about the interview, worried that he wouldn't do well. I tried to assure him he'd be okay. My son could charm a safe open, could talk his way out of hell—would that he'd turn some of that skill to study habits and writing papers.

The nearly pastoral campus of St. Andrews was the setting for the film **Dead Poets Society.** *The buildings have the look and feel of a monastery. Our guides, as I had requested, were two young Black students. St. Andrews is an Episcopal coed school. Boys wear ties and jackets. Mike's guide was from Brooklyn, my guide was from a town an hour away from the school. A thin, serious, young biracial student, he told me when I asked him about the racial atmosphere at the school that he felt more comfortable at St. Andrews than he had in the public schools. At St. Andrews, he told me, he wasn't teased by Black or white students as he had been in the public schools because he was biracial. And he spoke of finding a greater sophistication about the issue of race at St. Andrews than he had honestly expected.*

We toured the huge gymnasium and the indoor pool; I saw the science labs. The facilities for the students were expensive, impressive. After the tour, Michael had to write a short essay and then was interviewed; then the admissions director spoke with me. I was told that for the tenth grade, there are only five positions open. I'm not sure Michael will be accepted. During the drive back home, Michael marveled, "The boy who was my guide was pretty nice. I thought the kids there would be like robots or nerds." When we arrived home, the results of the SSAT test Michael had to take for St. Andrews and Westtown had arrived. I was almost afraid to open the envelope. He scored in the upper-fifty percentile, a good solid score. This score gives him a fighting chance at admission. But what does it really mean? Mostly that he is a product of an upper-class background and is familiar with the language—the jargon of standardized tests—and has a facility for testing well. It doesn't mean he's smart, and I reject it as a predictor of his future performance academically or in life.

FEBRUARY 13, 1993

Joe and I drove out to Mitchellville, Maryland, this afternoon to look at houses. We really want to stay in the city, but the cost of a house in a suburban-type neighborhood in Washington is simply astronomical. Mitchellville is quiet and clean, with lots of Black folks. Has been profiled in the N.Y. Times and on local news programs as an upper-middle-class haven where Blacks supposedly purposely choose to live rather than with white folks. Joe and I just want a large house we can afford in a clean, relatively crime-free neighborhood, and despite the media implications, I'm sure that's all most of the Blacks who live out there want. Little do white folks know that we really don't eat, drink, and sleep their perceptions of us, or tailor the most important things we do as a reaction to them. I've spoken with people who live in Mitchellville who say it is quite racially mixed. But for the media pundits and observers, the sight of so many well-off Blacks in one place raises the "self-segregation" or "conspiracy" bugaboo. As we drove around developments with names like Paradise Acres and Lake Arbor, Joe wondered aloud, "Now tell me what these people do wrong. Everybody always talks about the Black middle class selling out, not giving back to the community. What is their crime? That they get up and go to work every morning and stay out of trouble?" We talk often about the way in which middle-class Blacks are lambasted by other Blacks for their success and how whites cite that success as proof that racism is dead. I "give back" as part of my own political and spiritual lifestyle. But why can't just living a decent life, raising a morally sound family, be considered giving back too?

The homes are large, we saw several couples out jogging or walking together to stay in shape, and people waved as we drove past.

FEBRUARY 14, 1993

Michael turned fifteen today.

FEBRUARY 15, 1993

Tonight Michael and Joe had a standoff. The issue was the sloppy condition of the bathroom after Michael has been in it to shower or bathe. Michael gave Joe The Look and edged almost nose-close to Joe. Joe warned Michael to be careful and then simply pushed him away. Michael left the room. Joe refuses to lay a hand on Michael as punishment, saying simply, "I don't want to do that." I hear in his voice the hint that if he ever did, even with my approval, something might change between him and Michael so unalterably for the worse that he does not want to risk it. Joe has worked with young people all his professional life and tends to put more faith in imposing discipline and in reasoning than in physical punishment. He is my husband, but he is not Michael's father, and he knows this in a way that I sometimes choose to forget. I've talked with stepparents who've acknowledged that bonding with a stepchild is neither easy nor inevitable.

FEBRUARY 17, 1993

After school today, Michael and I took the train to Philadelphia. Tomorrow is Visitor's Day at Westtown, a full day of activities and programs for students applying to the school. Because the day will be so full, I wanted us to get a good night's rest rather than have to get up so early to drive up from DC. We'll take the commuter train to Westtown, thirty miles outside Philly, in the morning.

FEBRUARY 18, 1993

Woke up to find an inch of snow on the ground. The commuter trains to the suburbs were delayed. While waiting in the train station, Michael and I read **The Book of Questions**, which proposes various ethical and moral dilemmas and asks how you would handle each one. It was fascinating to hear Michael grapple with questions like, "Would you add one year to your life if it meant taking one year from the life of someone in the world selected at random?" Michael said no, vehemently. When asked, "If you could choose the manner of your death, what would it be?" Michael responded that he didn't much care about the manner of his death as long as he had "a chance to fight for it." I liked that answer a lot; listening to Michael, I learned that he is more thoughtful, and more brave, than I suspected. Today I remembered how and why there was a time when Michael may have been in some ways my best friend.

Westtown has a completely different atmosphere than St. Andrews. Here there is no dress code. And when we entered, the jeans, the fades, and the casual style of students made it feel like a regular high school. I was struck immediately by the multiracial and international character of the student body. Most of the Independent Schools have on average a 5 to 7 percent Black student enrollment. Westtown has 11 percent. There was a warmth, an openness, at Westtown that I liked immediately. Michael turned indecipherable during the visit, lapsing at moments into his "cool pose," so I could not tell what he was feeling.

We took the tour of the campus. My guide was a young Black girl from New York who told me, "I like Westtown a lot, especially because I don't have to play the role of the stereotypical Black for the white kids or the Black kids." That evaluation spoke volumes about

the kinds of identity conflicts our kids get wrapped up in and are
sometimes destroyed by.

After the tour, Michael was interviewed. Then I was interviewed.
During my interview, Susan Wiggins, the associate dean of admis-
sions, told me, "Your son just bragged about you being a writer; he's
so proud of you." I was surprised, for Michael never says anything of
the kind to me. I was honest about Michael's spotty record but was
assured that academic performance, while an important factor,
is not the only one weighed in admitting a student. Then I met the
headmaster, Tom Farquhar. We talked about how the school handles
conflicts between students. Disputes are settled through negotiation.
Fighting is simply not allowed. Students who fight are expelled. When
I asked what Westtown is looking for in the students they accept, he
said, "A student who will enhance what we have here, who will bring
something to the mix." Thirty-three states and nineteen countries
are represented in the student body. This is the school for Michael. I
have the feeling he will get in.

FEBRUARY 20, 1993

Michael wrote his father tonight. How will he and Femi relate to
each other this summer? What will they say? Talk about? What will
they feel?

• • •

African Americans exist in the imagination of America as a kind of
public property, suitable for endless, invasive examination and definition. Traditionally, white scholars have built lucrative, acclaimed
careers on analysis of our lives. Now it is the deaths of our sons that
foist us relentlessly into an arena designed by others, where our
sorrow and rage yield no protection against intrusion. We possess
no private racial space in which to mourn or regroup. Dissected, discussed, but still denied full equality or justice, we see our triumphs
and setbacks become the province where others ultimately reign,

armed with counterfeit knowledge we fail to combat. What will this unendurable loss of so many members of a generation mean? We are the ones who must speak, who must anoint this tragedy, give it a name, a designation that holds within it the path to a resurrection of spirit, hope, and resolve.

Three weeks before Christmas, 1990, when Michael was twelve, and three months after I met Joe Murray, Jay Bias, the brother of basketball all-American Len Bias, was killed, shot outside a suburban mall in Prince Georges County, Maryland. I was at the stove, preparing dinner, when Michael yelled, "Mom, Jay Bias has been shot." We knew the Bias family from the TV screen, had seen the majestic, eloquent mother, Lonise, transcend grief, seek meaning in the senseless, cocaine-induced death of her son Len, picked the day of his demise to play professionally for the Boston Celtics. We knew the father, James, sturdy, composed, less outspoken but obviously a bulwark of the family. We knew them. We knew them, my son and I, too well.

So, when I ran into the living room, still clutching a spoon dripping spaghetti sauce, and heard that Jay had been shot, I felt that because the media had connected me so intimately to the earlier tragedy and grief of the Bias family, I had lost one of my own. Jay died a few hours later, in the same emergency room at Leland Memorial Hospital where Len had died. The same doctors who watched Len's life elude their gifted hands and training saw Jay die too. Jay Bias was killed by twenty-seven-year-old Jerry Tyler, who fired into the Jeep that Jay was riding in with two friends. Two bullets hit Jay in the back.

This was the season of grieving Black mothers, their faces a somber mural possessing and filling the television screen, their stories a fixture in the morning papers. That is how I came to know them: Cynthia Harris, whose son was headed for college in Colorado before he was killed by a bullet intended for his buddy; Patricia Godley, whose fourteen-year-old son was killed in a Northeast alley; and Lonise Bias. Michael's vibrant, always-growing-right-before-my-eyes life symbolized the meaning and depth of these women's grief. In the face of their anguish and mine, I was a writer who did not know what to say.

I still did not know what to say when Michael asked over dinner a week after Jay Bias was killed, "Why are most of the people we see arrested on TV Black?" The food in my mouth suddenly lost its taste. I had taught him to relentlessly question everything he heard or saw, including everything his teachers said, and even to question me. In that moment I reaped my reward.

"Why?" he insisted, eating still, his eyes pressing me against the wall. My answer was a lecture about history, about "the system," and about sociology. I told Michael that some of the biggest criminals were shielded from discovery or punishment. And as I told him this, the unsatisfactory sound of the words clogging my ears, I wondered, what did slave mothers say to children who asked, "Why are all the slaves Black?" I had raised my son to believe that he could do or become anything he wanted. And I sat telling him that we were nevertheless prisoners of history. I could accommodate the contradiction. Michael merely gazed at me in confusion.

"Black on Black Crime," "The Black Male as Endangered Species"— the conferences, the studies, the books proliferated, mushroomed into a self-fulfilling prophecy, an industry that fed on itself. From 1987 to 1990, nearly 1,500 people, most of them Black males of all ages, were killed in Washington. And during this period homicide became the leading cause of death nationally among Black males aged fifteen to twenty-four.

What surprised me was that I didn't grow numb. I still felt horror and outrage at the violence and death—the teenage girl who fatally stabbed a young boy because he "joaned" on her mother, the infamous videotaped robbery and shooting where the perpetrators mugged for the camera and urinated on one victim. No, the victims didn't become faceless, nameless. I was wrenched every time.

A friend of mine, a counselor who kept track of such things, told me once that twenty-one was the most vulnerable age for young men. "Twenty-one," she said, "it's like if they can get past twenty-one, they'll make it." That's when more homicides, suicides, and accidental deaths occur among young men, she said. She told me this a decade ago. Len Bias was twenty-two. Jay Bias was twenty.

When Jay Bias was killed, in my role as Michael's mother, the what-ifs seemed never-ending. The questions began in the summer before he entered junior high school. There was the mad scramble to find a school that was not just academically sound but unplagued by gangs, violence, and fights. I thought in Backus Junior High we had found such a school. But I didn't breathe easy long. One of Michael's friends was jumped by a gang of boys at a Metro subway station near the school. He did a poor job of defending himself and was lectured by his parents about self-defense, manhood, courage. It was the same lecture I might have given in the past, but now I was afraid that the trigger of a gun pulled in a split second, the hairsbreadth slash of a knife, made such words irrelevant. And I sat dreading, waiting for Michael's first fight, a rite of passage once innocent, now fraught with the possibility of death.

In November, a boy from school started calling Michael in the evening, making verbal threats. I knew nothing of this until weeks after the calls began. Then, one afternoon, I was gripped by an instinctive urge to drive by Michael's school at three o'clock and pick him up.

All day I'd had a sense of foreboding, had been unsettled, on edge. I rounded the corner near Michael's school in time to see him heading away from the bus stop where he would normally board the bus for home. I saw his pumped-up swagger, his shoulders braced for battle, as he headed who knows where. He spotted me and halted dead in his tracks, embarrassed, angry that I had stolen his thunder. A quick interrogation revealed that he was headed to a nearby school and neighborhood to deal with the caller, who had labeled him a "chump." I ordered him into the car and we drove home, Michael fuming, me uttering a quick silent prayer that I'd caught him in time.

Pride and courage matter, and so my admonitions about nonviolence and negotiation rang hollow even in my ears. Joe and I talked to Michael that evening about contacting parents, about never going into unfamiliar neighborhoods alone to settle a score. As we watched Michael go upstairs to bed, Joe concluded, "He's got to defend himself, he can't let these kids walk all over him."

Joe had told me that whenever there was a murder on the streets or in the clubs of DC, the teenagers he taught at Dunbar inevitably knew the victim and the perpetrator. Having seen so many young men whom he had taught murdered in the past several years, Joe said he could now tell which ones wouldn't make it. "The ones who won't listen to anybody, who think they know everything, who've got a quick temper, they're doomed." And what of the innocent victims of these boys? Neither of us really wanted to talk about them.

So the next day, he told Michael, "When you're in public, watch how you walk. Don't bump into people. Don't stare. You're tall, but you've got an innocent face, and that sends a mixed message to people looking for trouble. People can tell you're a good kid just by looking at you, and they'll mess with you just because of that." The unscathed openness of Michael's demeanor was proof that he had been a protected, loved child. But this same quality was also suddenly a liability, one that he had to mask. As I listened to Joe lecturing Michael on how to present himself in public in the presence of other Black males he did not know, I was reminded of the admonition of Black parents in the South to their children to "never look a white person straight in the eyes." I thought, too, of the countless mannerisms and poses, of the complex ruses of language and speech that African Americans had fashioned over the years to maintain a sense of dignity while standing before the withering, unseeing glance of a white person who deemed them inferior. Now my son had to develop a vocabulary of body language that would serve and protect him in the midst of his own.

When I picked up the extension one evening and heard Michael say "shit" and "damn" in conversation with a friend, Joe told me, "He'd better know how to use those words sometimes. There are situations on the street and at school where knowing how to use those words could save his life."

In the spring, Michael joined Little League. The coach and his wife were dedicated to the adolescent boys they worked with three days a week and molded into a solid team. In the middle of the season, however, they played a game at a Southwest housing project, one of the city's toughest. During the game, the opposing team threatened to use bats on Michael's team if they were beaten. A neighborhood resident brandished a gun on the edge of the field. The spectators, rooting for the project team, became so threatening that the police were called to escort Michael's team off the field when the game ended in a tie.

In the months following the near riot on the baseball field, an insistent disbelief came over Michael that I was glad to see. I wanted him to be frightened when he should be, I wanted him to know that, even against the blood-drenched tapestry being woven from top to bottom in this society, violence and guns were not supposed to be the norm. I would have shuddered had the violence evoked in him absolutely no response.

• • •

I had wanted to meet Lonise Bias since the death of her oldest son, Len, had transformed her from a seriously religious suburban mother and bank executive into a charismatic, fervent evangelist on a crusade to save young people on the verge of trouble. And so, because I have always used language to try to explain the indecipherable, to heal and to transcend, I proposed a story on the violence racking the Black community to a local magazine, and for this story interviewed the Biases. When the television appearances began in the aftermath of Len's death, Lonise Bias's dignity, her anger, and her passion made me think that if Sojourner Truth or Harriet Tubman had lived in an era of mass media, they would have sounded like her. I wanted to meet her to discover how a mother says of her son's death, for a ten-second sound bite, "God took the best to save the rest." How many sleepless nights, how many tears, how many tranquilizers, how many prayers, bring you to the point where you can say that? God took the best to save the rest? I wanted to meet Lonise Bias because I wanted to know: How do you survive hell?

I knew that Lonise Bias thought that after Len died she and her family were safe. Fate, God, or whatever would never be so cruel as to take another one. I knew what the Biases had experienced, but I still wanted to know what pulled them through. For I had thought about Len as I watched Michael prepare for bed, and then I was thinking about Jay.

At the time of his death, Len Bias was a commodity, a valued asset of the Boston Celtics, the most historically successful and prestigious team in the NBA. Len Bias was a star. Red Auerbach, president of the Celtics, had said that no rookie player in Celtics history had ever inspired the anticipation that Len Bias sparked. Len had signed a lucrative contract to endorse Reebok athletic shoes. He was, at the age of twenty-two, a legend, and like all legends, he appealed to a kaleidoscope of wishes and needs in the collective psyche of a public that claimed and devoured him. He was the son of a devout, upstanding middle-class family; he was the "down" brother who, despite his dizzying talent on the court, remained accessible, popular, well-liked; a stylish dresser, he wore expensive suits as though born in them. A Black Horatio Alger, Len Bias was a success in a way that everybody could understand, and he was or would soon be a millionaire. On the basketball court, he was astonishing to watch as he turned the game into an art form. He was going to be the next great one. Already in the Promised Land, Len Bias was merely waiting for the rest of us to catch up.

On one level, the story of Len's final night was very simple. A group of young men gathered in a room in a dormitory at the University of Maryland to celebrate Len's contract to play with the Boston Celtics, signed earlier in the day. The young men celebrated with beer, cognac, and an ounce of 88-percent-pure cocaine.

Len's death is symptomatic of a culture that glamorizes chemically altered states while paying lip service to fighting chemical dependency. That night, Len Bias's last night alive, is a commentary as well on youthful bravado and the invincibility the young feel is theirs by right. Len and his friends could just as easily have been white students at Brown or Berkeley. What was Len Bias a victim of? His own bad judgment or arrogance? For ultimately, Len Bias chose to celebrate his victory with drugs and alcohol. Not all of his fellow teammates indulged. He could have, as his father hoped, spent that night at home with his family after they arrived from Boston on the shuttle. But he did not. One of Len Bias's closest friends, Brian Tribble, was with him the night he died. It was Tribble who frantically dialed 911 when Len collapsed, unconscious. The following year, Tribble would be acquitted of charges that he had provided the cocaine that allegedly caused Len Bias's death. Yet in the fall of 1993, Tribble, long known on the streets as a mid-level drug dealer, would be sentenced to ten years in prison for his role in a major cocaine distribution ring that operated in Washington, Maryland, and Virginia.

And what of Jay? Certainly, he was much more than Len's younger brother. Jay was, in his mother's words, "the one who's suffered the most because of Len's death." Jay graduated from Northwestern High School, where, like Len, he was a star on the school's basketball team. Although he was highly recruited, Jay failed to get the necessary 700 points on the SATs, which made him ineligible for a Division One scholarship. So he attended a junior college with a strong basketball program. He left after a year to work and to consider a four-year college and was thinking of entering American University. But his application to AU was turned down because he lacked sufficient transferable credits. Friends say Jay was losing interest in basketball. He had worked, upon returning home, in the dining facility at the Collington Episcopal Life Center in Mitchellville, Maryland. And he worked, at the time of his death, in the mailroom of a local bank.

How was it to be Jay Bias, Len's brother, when Len was alive? When he was dead? The wife of Jay's killer alleged during her husband's trial that Jay had been pursuing her romantically for months and that his attentions bordered on harassment. Jerry Tyler said that was why he shot Jay, to keep him away from his wife. Jay's friends said that Jay's last words before he died were the Lord's Prayer and a plea for them to tell his parents he loved them.

Did Jay ever dream of his own death? I am sure he dreamed about Len. What were his secrets? What were his fears? At twenty, Jay Bias must have wanted more than anything to find a way to be a singular, brazenly bright light, unconnected to the trail left by his older brother. At twenty, I am sure he only wanted to be Jay. But what we remember is that he died too soon, just like Len.

When Lonise Bias became a national figure, an overnight spokesperson on the plight of the nation's troubled youth, inevitably there was a postponement of the grief that she and her family felt. The process of grieving over the death of a loved one consists of days that go on forever, unfamiliar sorrows, the desire to be touched, held, listened to, the need simply to be left alone. In reaching out to the white, Black, brown, and yellow children of America, magnificently shaping her pain into an altruistic impulse that could only be admired, did Lonise Bias unknowingly deny Jay the chance to privately mourn, aided by her considerable compassion and skill? The turn outward, the move into the public sphere after Len's death, made sense of the senseless. Might a move inward, a closing of ranks and the family circle, have strengthened Jay, enabling him to grieve and grow and to more clearly find his own way?

It was imperative for me to meet James and Lonise Bias. We owned their son Len, whose triumph and death became public spectacle and process. So, too, in the same manner did we own their grief. But I wanted mostly to meet the Biases so that with them, I, too, could mourn—mourn with them the loss of two sons whose deaths had made me hold my own son closer. Our community, scrambling for answers and safety, unsure and under siege, lost resources, intelligence, and hope in the instant of Len and Jay Bias's deaths—as in the instant of all such deaths. I sat with the Biases as the Jews sit shivah, as grieving African mothers pray and offer food to carved wooden dolls representing their deceased children, I sat with them to speak the names of their two sons, to never forget.

The Bias home was located on a quiet, well-kept street in Landover, Maryland. James Bias greeted me at the door. He is a dark-hued man, friendly, easygoing, and solid. We sat for a few minutes, breaking the ice in the tastefully decorated living room. We discussed the weather—it was May and yet the temperature blazed like August. I didn't know what I expected, but not this peace, the tranquility that filled the spotless house.

Lonise Bias came upstairs from the basement. She is a tall woman who wears her height gracefully. They had just returned from a vacation in the Bahamas. An easy camaraderie, an emotional synthesis, joined this man and woman, honed during more than twenty years together. The death of a child is supposed to destroy a marriage. James and Lonise Bias sat before me, the strength of their union palpable, living, breathing in the room with us. The interview began with a prayer initiated by Mrs. Bias. I rose from the sofa in response to her outstretched hand, her tall frame filling the living room's space. We stood with our hands clasped while the sonorous voice of Lonise Bias sought divine intervention in what would pass between us. By the time I sat down, I knew how they had pulled through. They were born-again Christians possessed of a bedrock faith relevant to every aspect of their lives.

Since Len's death in 1986, Lonise Bias had lectured at colleges and high schools in forty-seven of the fifty states. She showed me a stack of letters from students and administrators praising her talks, giving her credit for turning young lives around. There was skepticism from some at first, she said. "What do you know?" they asked. "Your son was an addict." She does not accept this conclusion.

But the death of Len gave her a vision, she said, forced her on a mission to reach young people and their parents before it was too late, before drugs and violence filled a void parents feared to approach. And who was better qualified than she to speak? she reasoned. Her talks mixed a back-to-basics approach with a willingness to listen to and hear her young audiences. When she first started the lectures, she found that after she talked about Len's death, the young people lined up by the hundreds wanting to talk to her about a host of problems unshared with parents or other significant adults in their lives. So the letters, the hundreds of one-on-one conversations, had taught her what she called the six lies young people in America live by, the same lies that derail them.

Her voice whirring up like an engine, Lonise Bias ticked off the lies on each finger: "If I get all the material things, I'll be okay. If I join the right group, I'll be okay. If I do what the group is doing, if I disrespect adult authority, if I have sex, I'll be okay. No one has a problem like mine."

I sat rapt, as enthralled by Lonise Bias's presence and conviction as the hundreds of young people she had addressed. I realized that she was conducting a ministry, that she had been called to speak and to guide, and, that like all healers, she had tapped a spiritual genius that awaited her obedience and her touch.

The young friends of both Len and Jay still filled the house, stopped by to visit, bringing their girlfriends, their children. "This house is never empty," she told me. "It's always filled with young people who loved Len and Jay."

Of the past and the present, she said, "For twenty-two years we were just an average family, raising our kids to be the best they could be. We were close-knit. Nothing we experienced came close to this. I didn't realize what a problem drugs were until Len died. God strategically prepared me with a certain strength to go through all this. This isn't strength that's rational or that comes from man," she said.

Still, there was disbelief. James Bias said of Len, "You never imagine your son could die on a college campus."

In the days following Jay's murder, James Bias appeared publicly on Capitol Hill testifying in support of the Brady Bill and held a news conference with Jesse Jackson in support of gun control. I heard it more in the voice of James Bias—what had been lost here, the price the family had paid. I wanted to inquire, but found myself unable to ask how the two other Bias children, Michelle and Eric, had handled this double loss.

Gerald W. Eiland, the driver of the car from which Jay was shot, had been sentenced the day before our meeting, and I asked them their feelings. "I felt no vindication," James Bias said, shrugging. Lonise Bias said, "It's all a waste when a young man is sentenced to thirty years." What neither of them said was that even a life sentence wouldn't bring Jay back. And that they were still sentenced to a life without him.

(In the spring of 1993, a Maryland Appeals Court overturned the conviction and the life sentence of Jerry Tyler and the thirty-year sentence of the man who drove the car from which Tyler had shot Jay Bias. The court ruled that the prosecutor had violated the state's equal rights law when he used peremptory challenges to bar women from serving on the jury solely because of their sex, reasoning that they would feel more sympathy for Tyler. Yet it was a jury of eight women and four men that convicted Tyler. In a retrial that took place by the end of the year, Eiland's conviction on second-degree murder and related handgun charges would be overturned by a jury that after three hours of deliberation found him not guilty. Jerry Tyler was found guilty of murder in his retrial in the spring of 1994 and sentenced to a prison term of life plus twenty years.)

I closed my notepad and turned off the tape recorder, and the conversation drifted to where we as a nation and as a people were headed, how things had gotten this bad, who bore the blame? James and Lonise Bias and I talked of pride, crime, family, and the days before integration when segregation enforced a cohesiveness and a unity purchased with other political rights. We didn't long for those days, but wondered at the unevenness, the bitterness, and the dissatisfaction of the exchange. Before I left, we stood once more in prayer.

· · ·

The Biases were children of God, good citizens. What more, I knew they might ask, was there to be?

· · ·

FEBRUARY 23, 1993

This afternoon Michael went to the movies with two friends. Before he left, I gave him the lecture I have learned from Joe, told him how to handle himself in public. He is growing so fast that he is suffering growing pains in his arms and legs and does not know how to handle or control the body sprouting faster than he can adapt to it. I told him if he and his friends went into any stores, to stay in plain sight of the salespeople and to leave any bags they enter with at the counter.

FEBRUARY 26, 1993

Tonight I was called by a parent of a Westtown student who lives in Reston, Virginia. The school asked her to call me to discuss the school parent-to-parent and to answer any remaining questions I might have. She was affable and pleasant, and we shared adolescent war stories. Her son is a year older than Michael, likes Westtown, and has done well there. Near the end of our conversation, she mused, "But you know, sometimes I'm a little afraid, he's up there in the woods of Pennsylvania, anything could happen." Little did she know how eager I am for Michael to attend a school in a setting like that. For on the streets of our neighborhood and in the halls of Michael's school the "anything" this mother merely fears and cannot name is a reality we know too well.

MARCH 3, 1993

We looked at a house in Mitchellville today. It needs a bit of work but is large. Once we give it a paint job and put down hardwood floors, it will be perfect. Joe is leaning toward putting a contract on it.

MARCH 4, 1993

Joe and I went to dinner tonight with Steve and Carol, and I described my frustration with Michael's behavior in school and his grades. Carol said that Michael sounded a lot like their son, who has a learning difference called attention deficit disorder (ADD) which results in an inability to be attentive for long periods, forgetfulness, and poor performance of rote assigned tasks. She suggested I get a diagnosis from a doctor at the National Institutes of Health, a Dr. Alan Zametkin, who treated her son and is a leading specialist in research on ADD.

MARCH 5, 1993

Michael's "girlfriend" called this evening. As far as I know, it is a telephone and school romance. If there have been dates, I don't know anything about them. In the age of AIDS and STDs, I'm glad that the phone is their most potent form of communication. I have never met her. Know only her name—Sophia. I wonder what my son finds attractive in a girl? Has he had his heart broken yet? Will he be a generous thoughtful lover/husband/friend to women?

MARCH 9, 1993

Joe and I went to a movie this evening, took the subway. On the way back, at the Metro Center stop, we met a former student of Joe's. Joe has taught preschool, junior high, high school, and adult education in DC for the last twenty years. And we regularly meet former students when we are out, for he has helped to educate a generation of youngsters in the city. The young man we met was a student of Joe's when he taught at Lincoln Junior High School. The young man was well built, friendly, open, and there was a deference, a respect he accorded Joe and me that I don't often see in young people. He has graduated from high school and is studying to be a member of the DC police force. When Joe asked him about Lonnie, Melvin, Antoine, and several other boys who were in the class he taught with this young man [as a student], to each name the boy said, "He's dead" or "He got shot."

Eight of the twenty boys that Joe had taught in that class have been killed in gang or street or criminal violence. Even Joe, streetwise and difficult to surprise, was stunned. We stood in the subway station disbelieving, shaken. "Well, how'd you make it, man?" Joe asked as the young man's train approached.

"I saw the others getting killed, and I decided I wanted to live, no matter what. I made choices different than theirs," he said.

As we watched him board the train, smiling and waving goodbye, I wondered if it really was that simple. I know for some it is, but for others who live in neighborhoods so violent they'd be fools not to carry a gun, the choices are a conundrum. And standing beside Joe, who was still shaking his head in amazement, I remembered the former female student of his we'd met a few weeks earlier who told Joe about the students in her class. "Mr. Murray, the girls got babies and the boys are dead."

MARCH 11, 1993

Michael received a letter from Femi today; enclosed was a photo of his four-year-old son, Yemi. The boy has a strong, almost fierce personality that I could almost feel as I looked at the picture.

MARCH 25, 1993

We heard from St. Andrews. Michael's application was rejected. He didn't seem too upset. I think he wants to go to Westtown, though he will not admit it.

APRIL 5, 1993

An admissions officer from Westtown called today and informed us that Michael has been accepted. He has fought and resisted this outcome, and yet when I told him and we talked, he could not conceal his pride.

APRIL 7, 1993

It's been a month since Carol suggested I contact Dr. Zametkin. He sent me a packet of diagnostic forms for Michael's teachers to fill out describing his behavior in school, answering questions about attentiveness, completion of work, disruptiveness. But the teachers I gave the forms to two weeks ago filled them out as though they were recommendations for college; they praised him to the skies and downplayed all the problems they have complained about to me. I nearly wept when I collected the forms from the teachers. I had fully explained what the forms were, why we needed them. But they are simply of no use, no value, and yet they remain the primary evidence used in diagnosing the disorder. Michael's teachers are so burdened with huge classes, paperwork, bureaucracy, it was all I could do back in February to get them to write the recommendations for Westtown for him. But I feel especially frustrated because if ADD has been hampering Michael's ability to achieve, I want to get on with the diagnosis and treatment strategy. But I will wait until he enters Westtown and get the teachers there to assist in the diagnostic process.

APRIL 9, 1993

Joe and I took Michael to dinner and a movie tonight to celebrate his acceptance at Westtown. It was a good evening, we were all relaxed, easy with one another. Joe beamed in pride and could not resist a friendly lecture not to "blow" this opportunity. While we waited for our order, we congratulated Michael with a toast. As he placed his glass back on the table, however, he said, "Now I just have to make it through the summer without getting shot."

APRIL 28, 1993

Today was my birthday. Joe and I closed on the house in Mitchellville, and one of Michael's friends died of a gunshot wound, allegedly while playing Russian roulette.

Adedayo Ayodele and his family lived next door to us when we lived in an apartment complex in Northeast near Catholic University, in the days when Philip was a part of our life. His parents were Nigerian, and I remember "Adayo" (his nickname), which everyone called him, as a terribly smart, very aggressive, but troubled young boy who had been kept back twice in school and was frequently suspended because of fights. I remember, too, that the neighborhood kids teased him because he was very dark and because he was

African. This is the second boy whom Michael knows from the old neighborhood where we lived for five years who has died a violent death. A year ago, a young boy named Rico who had attended Backus with Michael was killed three blocks from his house on his way home from a New Year's Eve party.

When we talked about Adayo's death today, Michael said when he approached the school steps this morning, he saw some friends outside and they said, "Hey, man, guess what?" He told me, "I thought, 'Oh no, not Adayo, don't tell me.' And then they did, they told me Adayo was dead. I cried."

All evening Michael was upset, confused. "It makes me feel like if God could just take somebody like that, He could take me," he said.

There was an assembly at Michael's school this morning to deal with the students' feelings about the death of Adayo. Michael is angry that no one can explain to him why this happened. How do I tell Michael that God did not take Adayo's life, that Adayo, if he indeed was playing Russian roulette, put his own life in danger. But the story sounds very strange to me. I told Michael that whoever owned the gun bears responsibility too. But at this moment I think it is easier for Michael to believe that "God did it."

As Michael was packing newspapers for recycling tonight, as he washed dishes, we talked about Adayo.

"God created us with free will, Michael."

"Yeah, tell me anything." He shrugged bitterly. "God let this happen!" he shouted. "That's what you mean by free will. God let Adayo be killed."

"I don't know, Michael," I said, reaching to hold him, to verify and confirm his life in my arms. "Maybe that is what I mean, maybe it's all I can say."

APRIL 30, 1993

Michael told me that at school today two of the boys involved in the incident with Adayo told him the Russian roulette story was a lie.

Apparently Adayo and several other boys, all on suspension from school, were in the home of one boy playing video games. Another boy came into the house and brought out a gun to show them. When he put it close to Adayo's face, the gun fired. No one knows if it was an accident or murder. The boys told the police they'd been playing Russian roulette as a cover story. I feel in some ways as empty inside as Michael. I lived next door to Adayo and his family for five years. And I have tried to compose some words to say to his mother. What can I say when I feel so ashamed, so angry? I feel ashamed remembering how the boys in the neighborhood, according to Michael, teased Adayo relentlessly about his name, calling him a "dirty African," calling him "Black" and "monkey." (These same boys and children at school had teased Michael so much about his Nigerian name, Akintunde, that he begged me to let him use Michael as his first name.) I feel angry that the culture of violence in America made this boy less safe in what his parents literally viewed as the land of opportunity than he would have been on an unpaved road or in any home in any part of Nigeria, an allegedly "less developed" country. I called Backus and got the address of the family and sent them a card. The thought of hearing this grieving mother's voice was too much. I am not as brave as I thought I was.

MAY 12, 1993

I am in Yellow Springs, at Antioch. Tonight I called home, and Michael and I talked about his prom for graduating ninth graders, which is tomorrow night. Joe will take him and Sophia to the dance and pick them up. I wish I could be there.

. . .

A sometime mentor and friend, Joseph Jordan, director of Antioch's newly established African-American studies program, arranged my monthlong residency at the school when my classes at George Mason ended for the semester. Like many African-American professors on white campuses, Jordan served double, sometimes triple, duty as professor and as surrogate parent, counselor, and friend to the Black students at Antioch. The office of the African-American studies program had become an unofficial home base for Black and other students of color.

Again and again during my visit, when I asked, professors and administrators at Antioch told me there was no "typical" Antioch student. "They come from all over, and their backgrounds range from the old monied to the persistently poor," one colleague said. But with their studied casualness, and with the desire of most of them to work in fields that would allow them to change or at the very least impact society and the world, Antioch students were a special breed.

In my writing workshop, the students wrote about pivotal men in their lives. I was amazed that when given a chance to write about themselves, the class chose instead to consider and rediscover fathers whom they had never met, or who had died too soon, or from whom they were estranged; or a son who, in a moment that may never be understood or overcome, took his own life.

The only male in the class was a young man named Marc, who was the most sophisticated and ambitious writer. At twenty, he was wiry, thin, ebony-hued, and wore a nose ring. He brought to the first class copies of a long prose poem about his mother, a work that he would in the weeks that followed transform into a fierce and simply brilliant essay on his father, and on himself.

The poem, one of many he had written, was too long and awkward in parts, but I knew immediately he could write. When I told Marc this after the first class, he looked at me in genuine surprise, shifting uneasily as he stood before me, the eyes behind his Ben Franklin lenses uneasy, disbelieving. I recognized the look. I had seen it before on the faces of so many young Black students, so bright and so sharp that they were almost dangerous, and yet they simply did not believe this. So I told Marc to come to see me during my office hours. The words he wrote on paper had pulled me into the seams of his life. I wanted to know more.

The relationship I developed with Marc during my weeks at Antioch, becoming friend as well as teacher, reflected my style of teaching and evidenced my own hunger to hear a sensitive, articulate young Black male voice. For back home in Washington, Michael woke up many mornings a stranger to me. The house crackled with tension as he struggled with me and Joe to wrest identity, autonomy—life, it seemed, sometimes—from our sphere of influence. I talked to Marc hoping he heralded the future voice of my own son.

The youngest of three sons, Marc grew up in a Philadelphia neighborhood called West Oak Lane in Germantown. He was unashamedly devoted to the mother he credited with keeping him out of trouble, and maybe even alive, by encouraging him to read and stay off the streets. The father he admitted had bequeathed him his humor, playfulness, and dark skin was a source of anger, anguish, and discomfort, their conflicted relationship fueling much of Marc's best writing. In his spare time that semester, he was reading Jack Henry Abbott's rage-filled scream from behind prison walls, *In the Belly of the Beast*, and George Jackson's prison diary, *Blood in My Eye*. He admired both men, he said, because of their intellectual transformation behind bars. One of his cousins, Andrew, had been jailed in Pennsylvania, and the writer in Marc was eager to know what his cousin endured and how he could survive and possibly come out a better man. When he visited me in my office, we talked about crime, about punishment and redemption, the standard definitions of each and the definitions that life, unpredictable, often unjustly imposes.

During one of our many conversations, Marc told me that his SAT scores and high school grades were unimpressive; as he told me this, I thought of the fraudulent measures of this society for gauging intelligence and worth. I remembered, too, the bitter joke Joe had told me that asked: How does a Black college athlete raise his SAT scores? Answer: By checking white on the box marked RACE. Joseph Jordan and Elaine Comegys had told me that Marc's adjustment to Antioch had been rocky and his evaluations (given at Antioch in lieu of grades) inconsistent. But like me, both felt that when this young man became a "finished product," he would be awesome.

Marc and a close friend, Ren, also from Philly, arrived at Antioch born-again Christians. His mother was a devout Baptist, and shortly before coming to Antioch, Marc renewed his faith, even vowing to be celibate until he married. But after a year and a half on campus, he had found his views of faith, morality, and religion evolving and changing, sometimes radically. Time alone spent reading and thinking, conversations with other students, and especially traveling around the country meeting and working with people from different backgrounds—travel facilitated by the Antioch system, which combines academic semesters on campus with off-campus work experiences called "co-ops," which take students all over the country—all conspired to challenge and revise the orthodoxy of his faith.

Marc and I discussed the final draft of his essay during a session in my office one afternoon. I suggested several minor changes and edited the manuscript with him watching over my shoulder. His essay rivaled the work of some of the graduate students I taught at George Mason University full-time. Then we talked, as we frequently did, about books and reading, the process, the joy and discovery of it all. The weather in Yellow Springs had been fickle, and that day it was chilly, overcast. My small office was damp as a cave. My wall-length window revealed the campus, green but sodden from three days of rain. The class had already met for the last time. I would leave the next day. In this conversation with Marc, I asked him to tell me about his past, his present, and even tried to nudge him into the future.

"Did you miss hanging out on the streets with the other kids as a child?" I asked. "I was pretty scared to hang out with them. I just had this intuition. I knew, for example, if I hung out with my brother's crowd, I was going to get into something I didn't want to get into."

"What was happening on the streets?"

"Break dancing, turntables, and rapping. People would do that and get together on the corner. There'd be house parties, street parties. But I wasn't interested, so I went out with my small group of friends. And we'd always have to be headed somewhere. We couldn't just hang out on the corners, because just hanging out, there was always the possibility of trouble."

Marc spoke of "trouble" as easily, as banally, as Michael described the invasion of his school by armed thugs. Marc's voice was flat, unemotional, as though "trouble" were something that, at twenty, he knew and no longer feared.

Marc told me that his brother Corrie had been "in more trouble than he's willing to tell me about," and had been part of a group whose worst members had killed men and were now in prison. Corrie had been lucky, Marc said, for he was never involved in any criminal activities, although he was prepared to take the blame for a friend who beat up someone on the subway. "He was going to take the rap for this guy. I don't know how he got out of it, but he did. My mother was pretty upset with him."

"Why do you think he was willing to do that?"

"Well. Corrie's friend assaulted a guy with a pair of nunchakus that belonged to Corrie. When the police came, the others had left and Corrie was the only one on the scene, with the nunchakus in his hand. He didn't want to be a snitch. The charges were later dropped."

"Any other reasons?"

"I know some of those guys, and my brother and them had been in fights together and they had each other's back. And when you're in a situation like that, I guess you kind of fall in love with your friends, you feel they must be your real friends. But that's an illusion."

"Do you ever feel endangered?" I asked, wondering how young Black males responded to such labels.

"When I was growing up, I always felt a fear of hanging out in the street. I know," he said quietly, "that I felt fear. And I wasn't really thinking about the future."

At Antioch, Marc's horizons had expanded considerably, stretching far beyond what he viewed as the claustrophobic hold of his Philadelphia neighborhood on his sense of possibilities. Marc's co-op assignments had included working at the Amos House soup kitchen and homeless shelter in Providence, Rhode Island, at a shelter for teens in San Diego, and at a group home for autistic children in San Francisco.

"Tell me about the co-ops, what were they like?"

"When I went to some of my jobs, I had dreadlocks down to my shoulders, not cut short like my hair is now. Usually I got the job, but some jobs, they didn't hire me with dreadlocks because of the myth that the hair is dirty. Things like that the school really doesn't tell you about. They expect you to learn that on your own. The jobs I think I will have in the future will probably be live-in residencies with disabled citizens. That's something I'd like to do. I may have some trouble with clients' families. They may be a little bit racist. I had a problem with one lady because I was a man; I don't know if it was because I was a man that she didn't want me taking care of her daughter in a home for autistic children. I might have a problem with that. Some families might not want a Black man to take care of their loved one."

When I asked about his fears for the future, Marc said that he worried less about himself than about his three younger cousins who lived in a tough area of West Philadelphia. Their stepbrother was jailed in Florida. And even then, Marc was unable to reconcile the crime for which his cousin had been imprisoned, shooting and paralyzing a man, with the soft-spoken cousin that he had always known. Several months later, when Marc and I spoke, he told me that his cousin, like his brother, had taken the rap for a crime someone else had committed. The maze of allegiances and loyalties that bound these young men to others so firmly that they would sacrifice personal freedom gave me pause, made me wonder who was really paying for what and what "crimes" each supposed "innocent" had committed, perhaps on his own. I knew that protecting family and friends was also a strong motivation in cases like the one Marc described. I wondered also what Michael would do if ensnared in a moral labyrinth such as this one, and prayed he would never have to make such a choice.

"You told me that you write your cousin Andrew in jail. When you write to him, what do you say?"

"I send him poetry, he sends me poetry. We were real close growing up, and I guess I'm trying to get back to that time and place with him.

I ask him a lot of questions about what it's like in jail. But he doesn't tell me much."

"What do you want to know?"

"Well, I guess I sort of want to be a witness in a way. I feel like no matter what I do, something could have happened and I'd have ended up where he is. But I didn't. I want him to know I'm with him. I don't know, maybe I'm not in jail because he is."

"And your cousins?"

"I worry about them because they're attracted to the street life. So I'm turning them on to drawing, giving them my old comic books to read and draw from like I did as a kid. The oldest cousin is getting turned on to African-American history. He's thirteen and just read *The Autobiography of Malcolm X*, and it really affected him. I'm proud of him. He even wrote a letter to President Clinton asking that Malcolm X's birthday be made a national holiday."

"You say you are afraid for your cousins, but you weren't afraid for yourself?"

"Well, yes, I wanted to get out of Philadelphia. I felt like if I was going to die, I didn't want to die there. I really wanted to leave. I was afraid I'd get caught up in the street life if I didn't. Several of my cousins are in prison. It's like in my family, with so many of the men, they either end up in the army or in prison, and I decided I didn't want to go either place. My oldest brother, Brian, he's trying to become a corporate lawyer, and he's getting married this weekend. I don't know, he seems like he's trying to forget the neighborhood. But he says he's putting a lot back into the community. His church does that a lot too, so I trust him."

A subtext of much of what Marc had shared with me in our conversations was his desire to be of use to his community. When I asked him about this, he said simply that he didn't want to forget the community, especially the poor. And yet it was important for him to leave Philadelphia, he said, because "I felt like I was in more spiritual danger than physical. I needed a broader view of my life. Philadelphia seemed to be all there was to my life."

We talked about his father, briefly, hesitantly, and while I watched Marc shift nervously in his chair as I probed him on this subject, I recalled the stunning, visceral scene in his essay describing a beating he received from his father after he broke one of the man's bowling trophies, how his mother came to his defense and his father began to brutally beat her as well. I remembered, too, how near the end of the piece, his father stuttered in rage at Marc as he arrived home from work one day, "You don't know what it's like out there, but one day you will." We even discussed his skin color, his voice tinged with regret as he acknowledged the years of self-hate that he had felt for having inherited his father's Black skin rather than his mother's lighter hue.

"I never really liked being dark," he said. "My brother and I used to stand in front of the mirror and compete to see who was darker. And all of us men, my father and my brothers, used skin lighteners."

Suddenly he was animated, as though this admission had charged and strangely freed him, and the words were coming fast, unselfconscious, in a steady stream. With an abashed laugh, he said, "It got so bad at the end I even put it on my ass. I put it on my knees. I put it on my toes. Put it all over my body. That's how bad I wanted to be light. My father had that hang-up too. I mean, like, I never went in the sun in the summertime. I stayed in the shade. I was scared of getting even darker. My fear of getting darker helped me stay in the house during the summer. The city gets violent then, so my fear of getting darker kept me in the house and out of trouble too. So I was, like, a hermit. You know, I just recently realized that I have never dated a dark-skinned woman, mainly because since I never liked my skin, why would I date someone who looks like me?"

I looked at Marc, still dark despite years of skin lighteners, and saw a strikingly handsome young man. The watchfulness of his eyes, the smoldering intensity of his demeanor, the grace with which he carried his lean body, all imbued him with a charisma of which he was, I thought, totally unaware. Yet his anecdotes sparked memories of my mother's family, which was rabidly color-conscious. Like Marc, I, too, had had to grow up and away from the influence of home and family, flirt with and find other values in order to begin to love my Black self.

"When did you finally realize you are a good-looking Black man?" I asked, grateful for the chance to stroke his ego, hoping that he knew I meant it, hoping, too, that he really believed it.

"Books I read, like Malcolm X and Black women writers, and I just started coming to terms with it. And talking to people here on campus, and my friends. Talking to other dark-skinned people and even light-skinned Blacks. It was funny, how one person wanted to be darker 'cause he felt he wasn't Black enough. I really couldn't talk to my family about this."

"Do you think of yourself as an American or an African lost in America?"

"I don't think of myself as an American, because I lack broad experience."

"What do you mean?"

"Like, I haven't been anywhere. But if I'm outside of America, like I'll be this summer, I guess I can see it for what it is. I mean, I can read about it, but in many ways it's like reading about a distant country, it's still an abstraction, and I'm inside that abstraction. But if I get outside of it, I can see it clearly. Right now, I haven't gotten the full feel of how or what it is to be an American."

"Well, that's an entirely justified answer, I think. Our experience has been so painful here, so ambivalent."

"And lots of times I feel angry 'cause I'm confused. The more I read and the more people I talk to about their experiences, the more angry I feel, and I just don't know what to do with this anger, so I just, you know, get rid of this energy through some sort of artistic channel."

Soon it was time for Marc to head to his next class, but before he left, I made him promise that he would continue to write. I hugged him and walked him halfway. I headed back to my office alone and thought of his two brothers who had escaped the fate of their friends, and who, like Marc, were forging themselves into adults who could carry their own weight.

I admired Marc's compassion for others, his willingness to look deep inside himself even when, and especially if, it hurt. I hoped my son would one day have those qualities. I hoped he had them now. All the way back to my office, in my head I heard the mental tape of a conversation with a close male friend, Clyde McElvene, a man with whom I had worked on various projects, a Black man who was consciously struggling every day to challenge the traditional definitions of maleness and of race. One evening we talked about sons, and he said, "You tell a girl to be careful, you tell a boy to stay out of trouble. The irony is that this implies that the boy controls his fate and the girl is given hers. We live in a society that, day in and day out, perpetrates crimes against Black males, and we as a community never tell them that they are supposed to be protected."

JUNE 5, 1993

Joe is as excited about our plans to go to Nigeria as are Michael and I. He has talked with Femi's brother Bade several times on the phone and likes him a lot, has sensed the generosity and kindness in the man. This trip has been in the making since the day I sat down to write Femi. If I had not been prepared to stand on Nigerian soil again, I never would have written the letter. There have been times in the past three years since our reconciliation that I've thought it best to wait for Femi to come to the US to visit us. But the idea of me taking Michael to his father, to the place where he was born, yes, back to Africa, quickly rooted in my heart and displaced any other possibility. I have always known a journey back to Nigeria with Michael is the only meaningful way to close the circle of questions and longing my son will always carry until he sees his father. Michael seems unconcerned, relaxed, as the day of departure arrives. He said he told Moe and David that he was going to Africa and the idea seemed amazing to them. When he told them that his father was Nigerian, that he was born there, he said they acted as though he had said he was from Mars.

JUNE 8, 1993

Tonight I drove Michael's friend Demetrius home after they returned from seeing a movie at Union Station. When we got back home, we sat up and watched Arsenio Hall and Alfred Hitchcock reruns on cable. He told me about a paper he had to write for a project at the Male Youth Program. The paper was on Shaka Zulu, the South African warrior king. We sat eating popcorn and talked about leaders like Shaka, Stalin, and other men who could move, shape, and forge nations and history.

JUNE 14, 1993

Bade called this evening, elated over the results of the presidential election in Nigeria. Moshood Abiola, a wealthy businessman and philanthropist, won. He is a Yoruba and a Muslim, and Bade says he has learned from the family in Nigeria that Abiola won support from all regions of the country, a real triumph in a nation where tribal loyalties are as deeply entrenched as racial loyalty is here. The military ruler, Ibrahim Babangida, who has "run" the country since taking over in a 1985 coup, is scheduled to step down. I wish I felt as certain as Bade that this election heralded real change. I simply won't believe the military will return to the barracks until it happens.

JUNE 25, 1993

Talked with Bade tonight about Babangida's annulment of the presidential election results, alleging widespread voter fraud and misconduct on the part of the two parties, parties whose platforms he wrote and whose candidates he handpicked. Bade says he will be demonstrating in front of the United Nations next week with other Nigerians to protest the military's action.

JUNE 26, 1993

Michael and I got immunization shots for the trip to Nigeria today. And on the way back home, we stopped and got something to eat. I brought up the subject of our impending trip to Nigeria and asked him if he was anxious or nervous in any way. He said he wasn't. Then he said, "I wonder what I'd be like if you and my father had stayed together, how I'd be different if I'd grown up in Nigeria."

"Well, we'll find out in a few weeks."

"Was he a good man, my father?"

"Yes, he was, but there were things I needed that he couldn't give me."

"What things?"

"Well, you know how Joe and I talk a lot about things, talk about what we feel, how we spend time together, well, your father wasn't able to do that with me. He was closed a lot of the time. And I think his concept of what marriage was supposed to be was different because he was Nigerian."

"Well, then, what did you like about him if he was that way?"

"He was hardworking, ambitious, smart, and handsome, and there were times when he appreciated me and made me feel good, but we were just too different."

"You and Joe are different."

"But not on the most important things, not on the things that we feel we need from each other."

"Did my father have other wives?"

"No." I laughed. "I wouldn't have married him if he had."

We finished our meal and got back in the car and headed toward home. I confessed to Michael that I'd had difficulty sleeping the last few nights. I am not worried, but anxious, excited about the trip to Nigeria. I have not seen Femi in over a decade. A girlfriend told me she thought I was one brave sister to take Michael to Nigeria like this. She doesn't know how much I have prayed and meditated, hoping to bless our journey from start to finish, hoping to keep us safe, and hoping, too, to find for my son that the love I feared he had lost was intact, was still strong.

JULY 8, 1993

There were massive demonstrations and rioting in Lagos to protest the annulment of the presidential election results, with scores of people killed and hundreds arrested. I don't want to cancel our trip, but I will see how the situation looks when we are ready to leave. There is a sense in which political instability, nascent or active, is a fact of life in a country like Nigeria, but I am not willing to risk our safety, and Joe will not let me.

AN ACQUAINTANCE WITH GRIEF

Crime and punishment loom, twin, inescapable shadows on the landscape of African-American life. The most tenacious folklore of racism and European-defined history defines the Black man as a crime against nature. For centuries, it was criminal for an African American to learn to read, to escape slavery to freedom, or to compete in business with whites. The legacy of this censorious past includes punishment, the Scottsboro Boys, lynchings, a system of justice that metes out different punishments for Black and white, and prisons that warehouse Black men. So when a Black youth "gets in trouble," inevitably the pull of generations of dead weight, as well as an awesome déjà vu, color a mother's expectations and fears.

When I heard the knock on the front door that evening, I wondered if Michael had forgotten or lost his key. It was seven-thirty. Basketball practice at Shiloh, I assumed, had gone on later than usual. When I opened the door, I saw Michael clutching a plastic bag from Peoples Drugstore. A policeman stood on either side of him.

"Ma'am, is this your son?" one policeman asked, removing his cap almost apologetically as he spoke.

"Yes," I told him, standing in the doorway, utterly disbelieving what I instinctively suspected.

"Well, he was caught shoplifting in the Peoples Drugstore on the corner there. The manager called us to the scene."

"Shoplifting?"

"Yes, ma'am."

Michael stood, hunched and grim-faced, between the two policemen, avoiding my eyes. Before I could ask what he had taken, the policeman continued, "The manager told us that they'd suspected him of stealing before, and tonight they caught him. They let him go this time. Said they wouldn't press charges. But if he enters that store again, he'll be arrested."

"All right, all right, I understand," I told them. But did I?

"Goodnight," I said, watching them close the gate to our yard behind them as Michael brushed past me and slumped on the sofa.

I didn't know what to ask first—what he had stolen, or why. Michael clutched the bag from the store and sat stonily before me.

"Tell me what happened."

"I went in the store," he began in a tiny, cowering voice I had never heard from him before. "I had to buy some school supplies." He held up the bag as evidence. "And I had gotten everything I needed, pencils, pens, paper, and then I saw some baseball cards on a counter near the notebooks. I wanted them. I put them in my pocket. Then I went to the cash register at the front and paid for everything except the cards. When I was walking to the door to leave, one of the security guards stopped me. I denied it at first, then when they called the police, I admitted it."

"How much did the school supplies cost?"

"Five dollars and something."

"Did you have money for the cards?"

"Yeah."

"Why'd you steal them?"

"I don't know," he said.

"Had you tried to steal from the store before?"

"Only once. Small things, nothing big."

"Why?"

"I don't know."

I sat before my son, envisioning him behind bars at Lorton, Riker's Island, or Attica. Was this a youthful, fleeting burst of rebellion or the beginning of a career in crime? I knew that the "typical" shoplifter in America was a fortyish white suburban matron, not a teenage Black male. But at that moment, that hardly mattered.

I wondered where he had stolen from before and not been caught. Michael seemed as dazed, even confounded, by what had happened as I. There was no defiance; no bravado or even hostility. I sensed shame and something he would never acknowledge—relief.

My son knew right from wrong. And he knew that people paid for crimes they committed, especially Black youth.

"The size of what you took doesn't matter, Michael. Theft is theft, and at this moment you sit before me as a thief. You know you're lucky, don't you?"

"Yeah, I know that," he said in a hoarse whisper, shaking his head, still refusing to look at me.

Even as Michael sat before me, I saw the edge of a dollar bill peeking from his pants pocket. Had he felt in control, powerful, grown-up, at the thought of getting something for nothing?

"Michael, I don't ever want you to do something like this again. If there is a next time, the manager won't drop any charges, I'll see to that. And you know what that means.

"Go on upstairs and wash up for dinner," I told him.

That night, Joe and I decided to ground Michael for two months. Michael had come closer than he realized, and closer than I wanted to consider, to suddenly having a juvenile record. That thought frightened me as much as the fear that one day I might visit Michael in some jail, somewhere in America.

• • •

The case of Terrance Devonne Brown, a Roosevelt High School honor roll student and track star convicted of first-degree murder, infiltrated my life with a subtle, pervasive insistence. For a variety of reasons, I became interested in pursuing some deeper understanding of the seeming contradiction the case presented—the young man judged by some to be exemplary and by others nearly demonic—and of the mother who had raised him alone. The same day that Michael was notified of his acceptance by Westtown, Terrance Brown was sentenced to life in prison.

The shoplifting incident was three months old. And I reflected on the day of Terrance's sentencing that his mother, Ella Ross, and I had shared the hope that education would ensure our sons lived prosperous, productive lives. Ella Ross's hopes were now shattered. Mine remained intact. So it was love for my own son that drove me to decipher the puzzle and tragedy of the son of a woman I did not know.

Terrance had quietly stalked the periphery of my life, both as a former student of my husband's and as a mentor in Shiloh's Male Youth Program under the tutelage of Jake Roach, where Michael came to know him. During Terrance's trial for murder, Michael came home from Shiloh Baptist Church each evening in a virtual daze of confusion. Michael, like most of the youngsters in the program, could not fuse his memories of Terrance—well-mannered, thoughtful, friendly, and clearly favored by Jake, who cited Terrance's academic accomplishments as a standard the young boys should aim for—with the alleged killer Terrance was accused of being in a Maryland courtroom.

In time, Michael's anguish began to reflect the at first latent, then quite vivid curiosity I felt about the case. I wanted to know who Terrance Brown was on the night of April 16, 1992, the night when as he later admitted he had killed a man. I wanted to know who he had been before that night. One thing was clear and indisputable: Terrance Brown had shot and killed an off-duty policeman. The murder occurred in the midst of what appeared to be, and what a friend and alleged accomplice testified was, an attempted robbery. The murder took place the day before Terrance was to leave Washington to sign papers for a Board of Governors scholarship from Indiana University, a four-year college located in Pennsylvania. The oppositional, conflicting nature of the primary elements of the case initially seemed stunning, a young man with everything to lose committing an act that placed his future and his freedom in great jeopardy.

Christopher Ryan Johnson, a twenty-five-year-old Prince Georges County policeman, married and the father of a young child, was waiting for a friend outside the friend's home in Capitol Heights, Maryland. He stood in front of his car checking the headlights, and moments after a young man he did not know approached him, he was shot five times in the throat, back, and thigh. He died two weeks later. The young man was Terrance Brown.

I wrote about Len and Jay Bias in order to mourn. I interviewed Terrance Brown and his mother, Ella Ross, to try to comprehend the inexplicable. Mourning, I found, was in the end easier.

From the beginning, the case for the prosecution was simple: A felony robbery attempt had ended in murder. But the defense asserted that the case was as much about perception and misread signals as it was about the death of an innocent man. First of all, the defense asked, why would a young man with everything to lose like Terrance Brown choose to destroy a future more promising than anyone in his family had ever been poised to claim? Terrance Brown's defense was that he had approached Officer Johnson to offer assistance after he and a friend drove past and spotted Johnson's flashing hazard lights. Brown approached Johnson with a gun at his waist, a gun the defense said he carried for protection because of a violent feud with a classmate. Spotting the weapon and mistakenly assuming he was being robbed, Johnson began handing over his credit cards and money to Brown and then reached for his service revolver and fired at Brown, whom he wounded in the stomach even as he himself was shot several times. Brown, the defense argued, shot Johnson in self-defense.

The only witness to the events of that night was Harry Melvin Mayo, a classmate and friend of Terrance Brown's in whose car Brown had been a passenger. It was Mayo who drove a bleeding Brown to DC General Hospital for treatment and who called Ella Ross to inform her that her son had been shot. Court documents filed at the time of the arrest of both young men said that Mayo and Brown had spent the evening taking turns committing robberies. Under cross-examination, Mayo said that he had used his own gun, hidden beneath the seat of his car, earlier in the day.

Both young men were charged with first-degree felony murder. Mayo was picked out of a lineup by a man robbed twenty minutes before Officer Johnson was shot. And on the stand, Harry Mayo, who had declined an offer of immunity from the state prosecutor but who would later receive a more lenient sentence than Terrance, admitted being an accomplice to first-degree murder. He testified that Terrance Brown had approached Johnson with the intent of robbing him. In testimony that Michael Statham, the attorney for Terrance Brown, later said effectively sealed the case against his client, Mayo said, "Because somebody's father and son and husband was killed, I want to clear my conscience. I feel guilty about what happened."

Those with whom I spoke who had attended the trial said that Mayo, a more soft-spoken, seemingly less assured young man than Terrance Brown, was both compelling and convincing on the stand. Witnesses to the trial told me that Mayo's display of vulnerability, remorse, and compassion for the Johnson family (real or feigned) was more "winning" in its way than the steely intelligence and quick-witted articulateness of Terrance Brown, who presented himself, in the estimation of some observers, as "too smart" and "too confident." Two dozen character witnesses cited Brown's accomplishments, which went beyond the honor roll and the world of athletics. He had delivered food to the elderly as part of a youth program and in a twist of irony, had been proclaimed "best defense attorney" in a mock trial competition organized by the Georgetown University Law Center.

Ultimately, Terrance Brown was found guilty and sentenced to life in prison, plus ten years on gun charges. He would be eligible for parole in seventeen years but would then have to begin serving the ten-year sentence on the weapons charges. Harry Mayo pleaded guilty to first-degree felony murder, attempted robbery with a dangerous weapon, and carrying a concealed weapon. Mayo was sentenced to life in prison, but the judge in the case suspended all but fifteen years. The judge also said he would reconsider the sentence in ten years if Mayo demonstrated that he was a model prisoner.

The case of Terrance Brown cast a pall over the Male Youth Program, for Jake Roach had mentored and coached Terrance for several years, working with him first in the Mayor's Youth Leadership Initiative and then assigning him to mentor younger boys in the program at Shiloh. The two were so close that they often talked by phone several times a week about school, Terrance's weight training, and career plans. Jake Roach said, "When I met Terrance Brown, I saw a general, a physicist, a professor, and the second coming of a football star like Lawrence Taylor all in one person."

And it was Jake, along with Peter Parham, DC's then Director of Human Services and the father of Terrance's girlfriend, who accompanied Terrance when he turned himself in to the Prince Georges

County police after being released on bond by the DC police who had originally arrested him. That was a day that Roach described as "one of the most difficult days of my life."

At the sentencing, the judge sternly lectured Brown, calling him a young man who possessed two different personalities, one concerned and caring, one cold and manipulative, one personality for his family and one for his peers. If the judge's conclusions held even the smallest amount of truth, then Terrance Brown had effectively betrayed a virtual community of supporters, mentors, friends, and family. I did not know whether I believed Terrance Brown was indeed guilty of felony murder, as opposed to murder in self-defense. But I knew that the insurgent, cruelly baffling nature of the events that had resulted in Terrance's imprisonment struck a chord of fear within me for my son. Every mother wonders about the secret life, the hidden yearnings and fantasies, of her children, and whether they will control them or become victims of them. And so, long before I thought of talking to Terrance Brown, I talked to his mother.

• • •

Ella Ross is a tiny woman of impressive self-possession, and it was clear soon after I met her that her emotional investment in her son was the singular and most important force in her life. Terrance was not merely a son but a chance for her to erase the horrors of her own childhood. Through Terrance's achievements she had hoped to attain a kind of grace, as well as a redemption that even her own considerable achievements may have failed to invest within her.

As I spoke with Ella Ross over a period of several weeks, it became apparent that she had taken onto herself a large measure of responsibility for the incalculable, unknowable forces that had derailed Terrance from the neat trajectory toward success that had seemed to be propelling him until the night of April 16. Her guilt was enormous, and she was dogged by deep-seated feelings that she had "failed" Terrance. Even imprisoned, Terrance dominated his mother's thoughts and actions as totally as he had when he was free.

Ella Ross worked as an accounting technician with the Department of Health and Human Resources, where she handled all accounts for the secretary of the department. She had successfully defeated the pull of a multitude of degenerative forces in her life. Through hard work, persistence, and an impressive inner resilience, she had managed to create a succession of opportunities for Terrance. One of the most twisted, tragic ironies of the story of this mother and son is that while the mother rewrote and restructured the symbols that at birth seemed destined to define her, the son was ensnared by the full intent of their horrible grasp.

Ella told me that her childhood was marked by poverty, disruption, and dysfunction. Her parents fought violently and often, and when Ella was nine, her mother left her father and lived for a short time with her ten children in a public shelter before moving into an apartment of her own. But there were frequent moves around Northwest Washington in the aftermath of evictions for nonpayment of rent.

Her oldest sister, Ruby, became a surrogate mother for the family. Ruby was independent and strong and became a model for Ella. When she was thirteen, Ella met Harry Lee Dixon. She and her family were living in the Sursum Corda housing projects, located in a Northwest neighborhood. Ella met Dixon on a summer night through some friends. He was four years older than she, drove a car, was working, and, though married, was separated from his wife. To Ella, yearning for stability and security, he seemed mature and stable. Two years later, Ella dropped out of school and moved to New York with Dixon, where he had family. They moved into an apartment and began living together. Of that period, she remembered, "I felt like I had my own identity in New York with Harry. I was happy for maybe the first time in my life. He was working steady in construction, we had a nice apartment with nice furniture, and he took care of me."

Terrance was born in Washington when Ella was sixteen, and Dixon forged a relationship with his son that was enduring and strong, one that flourished despite the cycle of drug abuse, arrest, incarceration, release, and rearrest for drug selling that became the pattern of his life after he was injured in a work-related accident. The drug abuse led Ella to leave Dixon in New York when Terrance was five and return to Washington. "I had a sister who lost an eye to drugs, I have a brother who spent fifteen years in jail because of drugs, and my father at the age of seventy-two was jailed for drug pushing, so I just have always hated the idea of drugs," Ella said.

When she returned to Washington, Ella relied on her sister Ruby for help with Terrance. By this time, the combination of motherhood and her desire to have a better life than she had known as a child fueled an intense ambition. She worked at a fast-food restaurant and at night, while Ruby cared for Terrance, attended Armstrong Adult Education Center to earn a general equivalency diploma.

From the beginning, she recalls, Terrance was special in the family circle. "And I think I tried to make up for what I lacked. When he was a kid, I could go without a purse or without clothes, but Terry walked around in forty-, fifty-dollar suits. He had the designer shoes, and that's probably where I made my mistake. I just made sure that I did for him what was not done for me."

As Ella narrated the years as a single mother, the specter of her son, now behind bars, seemed to shape each word, infect the timbre of her voice. Terrance was alive, but he had killed another mother's son. He was alive, but when she saw him once a week, he was handcuffed. The one the family thought would redeem them all had somehow betrayed them instead. And so in every line of the narrative Ella Ross wove, she sought to find the reason why. Each possible answer pointed in her mind to an excessive, corrupt, damaging quality to the love she had offered her son. Yet she, who had been indifferently loved and protected, decided to perfectly love her own child. Denied adequate food, shelter, and clothes as a child, Ella Ross grew up and did what good mothers do a million times a day around the globe: She braved a chill and darned holes in her socks so her son could be warm. She had seen good mothers on television, in the movies, read of them in books, seen them in other families, and watched her sister Ruby, only a few years older than she, shoulder responsibilities her mother could not. She had never been effectively mothered, but Ella Ross knew what society said a good mother was.

"I went to all the PTA meetings," she said, "all the track trips. I was there, participating, taking pictures. I raised money. I did everything, like I said, that my mother did not do for us." In the midst of this conversation, she spoke of having spent four hundred dollars on clothes, shoes, and cassette tapes to send Terrance in jail. I saw that for Ella Ross, caring for Terrance had become an obsession and a need that fulfilled a sense of herself as capable, powerful, in control. I wondered when she would let go. I wondered if she could.

Her life as a single parent revolved around Terrance, including getting him to school on time each day while holding down a full-time job. When Terrance was in elementary school in Northeast, Ella was working in downtown Southwest. Without a car, and living on Alabama Avenue Southeast in one of the most isolated areas of the city, she boarded a series of buses in the morning and in the evening. Weekends, too, were devoted to Terrance, taking him to

Cub Scouts or Boy Scouts or to play with friends from school. During one conversation, Ella said that because Terrance was a boy, "in a way, I was kind of making it up as I went along. I didn't know how to raise a son. All my brothers were either in trouble or in jail. There was Ruby to help me, but she had girls." It may have been then that she began in a sense to live through Terrance, to make him the most important person in their world, and to willingly sacrifice, perhaps more than was required, in the name of a mother's love. The dedication seemed to pay off. Terrance was a bright student in school, one who regularly made the honor role, excelled in sports, and won scores of awards and trophies.

There was a five-year relationship with a man who cared a great deal for Terrance, but for Ella the affair was stormy and unsatisfying. And while Ella was struggling valiantly to keep Terrance away from negative influences, she was torn by the demands of his natural desire to know his father's family. And so Terrance often spent summers in New York with his paternal grandmother. Ella was frustrated, for at the end of the summer when Terrance returned to Washington, she heard in his speech and saw in his mannerisms the influence of weeks spent with tough, older, hardened street kids.

In 1984, Ella met Albert Ross. He was a bartender and was steady and capable, and he made her feel secure. But Terrance resented Ross, felt that he undermined Ella's loyalty to him, and Terrance resented his attempts to impose a stricter, more consistent form of discipline than Ella had. But four years after they met, Ella and Albert Ross were married. After their marriage, there were frequent arguments about how to discipline Terrance, and Ella admits that she was, as Albert noted, often lax and inconsistent in meting out deserved punishments to Terrance.

"When I told Terrance to wash the dishes, he'd wash them any old way. It didn't bother me too much because I figured I was going to wash them anyway," she told me. "I'd just rewash them. I didn't go into it with Terrance. My main thing was schoolwork. Don't let a teacher call me and tell me he wasn't doing his homework or that he was absent. Then he was in real trouble."

Because Ella saw education as the way for Terrance to erase the past they had inherited from her parents and from his father, a past of failure and dysfunction, she made education a kind of mantra, imbuing it with extraordinary powers to transform. Yet Albert Ross urged that discipline and standards be imposed on Terrance in all of his activities and responsibilities, and he saw a connection between poorly washed dishes and the rest of Terrance's behavior. Stepfather and son argued frequently, once or twice came to blows, and settled into occasional periods of peace. But for Ella, "It was like there was not enough of me to go around. My husband tried to pull me in one direction, Terrance tried to pull me in another direction. I thought having a baby would ease things, but it didn't." Ella named her newborn son Albert, Jr.

The tension between Albert Ross and Terrance mirrored other conflicts in Terrance's life and behavior. "Terrance figured, you know, he'd think if there's a problem, get out there with your fists and fight," Ella explained when I asked her about several fights Terrance was involved in. He had been transferred from Dunbar High School because of a fight, and while working with Jake Roach in the Mayor's Youth Leadership Initiative, escorting a group of children on a field trip one day to the Anacostia Museum, Terrance got into a fight with a young man and threw him through a glass exhibit case. Jake Roach fired Terrance but eventually accepted him back into the program. A few weeks before the shooting of Christopher Johnson, after gambling for money in a series of card games with a classmate at Roosevelt who refused to pay the five hundred dollars he owed, Terrance beat him up as a warning to pay the debt. And so the well-mannered youth, the bona fide scholar, the star athlete, held within him a tremendous wellspring of anger.

By the time Terrance was awarded the scholarship to Indiana University, his life was one of vivid, interminable splits. Ella had found it impossible to keep him away from his father whenever Dixon was released from jail. Yet for Terrance, Harry Dixon was simply and only his father, no matter what, and his loyalty and love for the man were fiercely resistant to his mother's warnings. Terrance was surrounded by a host of male forces. In Terrance's last year of high school, Albert Ross, who loved him, had formally adopted him. Ross struggled to be a positive force in his life, even as Terrance built barriers between them. Jake Roach was a source of advice and support, but there was also Terrance's increasingly close friendship with Harry Mayo. Terrance had also begun to spend more and more time at his grandmother's house, where Ella feared anything could happen and where so many of the influences she tried to protect Terrance from were often in the picture.

But in the spring of Terrance's senior year in high school, Ella Ross may already have allowed herself to imagine attending his graduation in June and to revel in fantasies of another graduation four years hence. For her son had traveled places she had never been; he could count on community leaders and members of city government for advice and references. Academic and athletic awards lined the walls of her apartment. The scholarship he had received covered virtually all his academic expenses. I am sure that during that spring, Ella Ross more than once flash-forwarded in time in her imagination, looked back, and concluded that the sacrifices, the conflicts, and the pain had all been worth it.

• • •

JULY 9, 1993

*This afternoon, Joe, Michael, Joe's son Austin, and I drove over to
Annapolis to have lunch with Aunt Bert. At seventy-five, she is a
marvel, in good health, informed, sophisticated, and travels so much
we can hardly keep up with her. If it is Paris, the Bahamas, or San
Francisco, Aunt Bert has been there, and often with a young niece
or friend or relative forty years her junior. We went to a family-style
restaurant. Around the table this afternoon sat four generations.*

*Aunt Bert has "adopted" Austin as grandson, as she did Michael,
sending him birthday and Christmas cards with money and stocking
up on toys in her apartment for our visits. Over lunch, the conversation drifted to developments and changes that marked the
differences between her generation and mine and between mine
and Michael's. As in all conversations of this kind, we adults were
pretty rough on today's kids. We talked passionately about the lack
of self-respect and discipline that we see in so many young people.
We talked about money, responsibility, the future.*

*I felt a little sorry for Michael, for he was outnumbered. But
the conversation, which had Aunt Bert recalling tough times in the
thirties and forties and how hard she had worked, and Joe com-
plaining about the failure of so many of his students to really apply
themselves, symbolized the fear that so many of my contemporaries
share, that our children will squander what we worked so hard to
gain. Sitting at the table today was my husband, who worked three
jobs in order to buy rental properties. For me, work and achievement
have been the way I have let the world know I am here. My dedication
to language and spending long hours working with words helped
pay for the house in Mitchellville and will pay for Michael's tuition
at Westtown. But Michael lacks fire, the hunger that drove many of
us even when we were his age.*

Where, we wonder, is the hunger in our kids that drove us? This quandary is not unique to African Americans, it is the story of any successful class or group—how to ensure that their progeny build on rather than waste what they have earned. But because each higher rung on the ladder is grasped despite so many obstacles, so much we have to overcome, refute, ignore, deny, the question of what our children will do with the dream rests at the heart of the matter.

Michael's response was simply, "I can't help it that I was dealt a lucky hand."

"It's not luck," I told him, "that results in you sitting here with us healthy, strong, smart, and endowed with advantages so numerous you take them for granted."

"You all talk about rap music being bad, and the clothes we wear, but it's you, you adults, who created MTV and who sell the music and make the clothes," Michael insisted vehemently, certain he had proved our collective hypocrisy.

"All right, we do make the jeans," Joe said, "but we didn't tell you to wear them down to your knees." He laughed, breaking the tension simmering among us.

"Listen, dear," Aunt Bert told Michael, patting him gently on the arm, "your parents and I just want you to carry on and do as good as we did or better."

. . .

At Roosevelt High School, they called Terrance Brown "Prime Time" because of his personality, his academic success, and his ambition. "Prime Time," as though he was already a star. But as I drove out to the Maryland Correctional Institute in Jessup to finally see Terrance Brown after having spent many hours talking with his mother, his lawyer, and Jake Roach, a multitude of thoughts unraveled in my mind and competed for my attention. I thought of the three different accounts of what had actually happened on the night of April 16. There were the rumors that had floated on the streets that Terrance and Harry Mayo had been, in the street vernacular, "doing the do"—robbing people at random—and that on the night of April 16, they finally got caught. I thought of Mayo's confession. Some argued that the confession was merely the untrustworthy narrative of a young man facing separate robbery charges who betrayed a friend to gain a lighter sentence. In any event, the jury clearly believed Mayo's version of the events of that night. Are guilt and remorse automatically erased from the emotional vocabulary of a young man because he may have committed a crime?

I thought as well of Terrance's assertion that he was a good Samaritan who had been mistaken for a thief, and I considered how people who knew him said such an act of assistance would have been consistent with the Terrance Brown they knew. However, I couldn't shake a friend's nagging question: "How could a young man who had never fired a gun before outshoot a trained police officer and hit him five times unless he'd already had his gun drawn first?"

And Ella Ross had acknowledged that "yes, a life has been taken, yes, some time has to be served," in the letter she wrote to the judge pleading for leniency, a letter that led the judge to sentence Terrance to ten years instead of twenty for the related gun charges in the case. I wondered if the confidence that Ella Ross had so lovingly instilled in her son had turned instead into a sense of invincibility that made him feel he could rob at will and head off to college the next day.

Terrance's lawyer, Mike Statham, talked with me about the trial and about Terrance; making Ella Ross a symbol of so many Black mothers, he concluded, "Our women have had to face so much. We are the only race on earth that asks our women to lead the race out of bondage, and they simply can't do that alone. I see so many Terrances, and when these Black boys are in trouble, they come into my office with their mothers. The mothers always come, the fathers are never there. And it's then that these women ask me to talk to their sons, talk to them the way some father, some man, should have long before they were sitting across from me. And often by then, it's too late."

Statham's words were heartfelt and clearly impassioned, but too neat, too unmindful of the complex, unruly task that parenting becomes in all families. Jake Roach talked to Terrance several times a week and saw him almost every day. Albert Ross had cautioned, had tried to intervene. These were no absent, indifferent, shiftless, or lazy Black men. Instead, caring, concerned adults wished for Terrance's success, even more than he did, if that is possible. And Ella Ross had led her son away from the bondage she had known, the bondage of poverty, the fear that you are not safe, secure, and loved. Ella Ross did everything right, yet somehow her son still lost in the end.

As I drove out to Jessup that day, I still did not know if Terrance Brown was a murderer or the victim of a more than cruel twist of fate. I did not feel any longer that awareness of his guilt or innocence was mine to search for or claim. But I still wanted to see if I could gain some small measure of knowledge about who he had been and who he was now. And I promised myself that would be enough.

We talked in a small room off a noisy corridor near the entrance to the prison. The first thing that struck me was how young he looked. Ella Ross had given me pictures of Terrance at different ages, and in all the pictures, I saw immediately his steely confidence; however, sitting across from me was a nineteen-year-old youth who was really still a boy. Very dark-skinned, tall, he wore a stylish shirt, with jeans that were fashionable and expensive. His smile was expansive, almost heartbreaking in its radiance. Terrance still had unflagging friends and supporters who visited him. Peter Parham, the father of his former girlfriend and an official in city government, still came to visit him regularly, he said, and girls from Roosevelt came to visit him too.

When I asked him how he was holding up in prison, he told me that to get through each day, he had tried "a little bit of everything. I've even tried yoga. Sometimes I laugh to keep from crying." When I asked if he had changed in any way since his incarceration, he said, "I feel more bitter, I don't trust people as much as before. I feel like it was a betrayal of trust that got me here. I mean, like, I feel betrayed by Harry, and even though I'm sorry that I killed that policeman, I went up to him with no bad intentions. He just assumed I did."

When he first arrived in the prison, because he was considered a cop killer, the other prisoners showed him a deference, a respect, that chilled and shamed him. "They let me use the pay phone before others, or threw me the basketball as soon as I walked onto the court," he said. I recalled Jake's judgment; during a phone call one evening when we talked about Terrance, Jake had told me, "Ironically, Terrance was on the top on the outside, and in prison there's nothing higher than a cop killer." His cellmate then was a young man Terrance had known as a child when he lived in Southeast. He was a year or two older than Terrance and had been sentenced at sixteen to life imprisonment for murder.

"They say everything happens for a reason, and I figure this has to be for something that I did when I was younger," Terrance said, explaining his incarceration. "When I was fourteen, maybe fifteen, my mother caught me selling drugs, and she put me out. I went to live with her mother. And the deal for me to come back home was that I couldn't sell any more drugs. From that point on, I made a 3.0 grade average and started volunteering and was involved in sports, the Mayor's Youth Leadership Initiative, and the Male Youth Program."

He started selling drugs, he said, "to strike back at my mother's husband. I resented him a lot and felt jealous. I'd feel so bad, sometimes I didn't want to ask him for anything." So he began hanging out with older boys in the neighborhood, going to clubs where his prowess on the dance floor earned him large tips from the hustlers who liked just watching him move. They'd give him as much as fifty dollars sometimes just to dance.

"So when I'd get upset about things happening at home, the guys in the street would say, 'Don't worry about it,' " Terrance explained. The sequence of events Terrance narrated was ancient, predictable, yet still tragic. It was a story we all in some sense know, yet hope we will never have to hear about one of our own.

"And so one day I went with one of them and told them I wanted a package, and that's how it started." As Terrance sifted through a host of memories, I sat across from him watching an impressive display of his confidence, still resilient despite his conviction. I heard how articulate he was; I felt his energy and knew why Mike Statham had said, "He could've been a politician, a lawyer, a doctor, anything he wanted to be, he was that smart."

Over and over during our conversation, Terrance spoke of fights and his prowess with his hands. At the Male Youth Program, he told me, "They tried to get me into boxing because they had heard a lot about my hands." In his Southeast neighborhood he was known as a good fighter, and now he wondered aloud if some of the young men who befriended him saw him more as an enforcer than as someone they liked, as he said, "just because I was me."

And what did the fights mean to him? "It was just that I was young and I could fight well, and in the neighborhood fights, you always need somebody to fight for the way."

Yet Terrance insisted that he was a loyal, supportive friend "unless you rub me the wrong way. But if you give me one reason to believe that you're against me or something, you don't want to be my enemy. If I'm upset enough or you've done the wrong thing to me, there's no other way for me, you understand? If I'm mad enough to put my hands on you, there's no way I'm gonna walk away."

From behind prison bars, Terrance has forged a relationship with Albert Ross that is intimate and trusting. Ella had told me that when Terrance called home from prison, he asked to speak to his stepfather more often than to his mother. Ella said she knew that the two men had written letters to each other, letters she had not seen but that she suspected laid a foundation for the new bond they had forged.

"Why now?" I asked. "Why not before?"

"It's just that when I was home, my head was the size of this room," he said, moving reflexively to gesture with his handcuffed wrists to take in the room's small circumference. "You couldn't tell me anything because I thought I already knew it all. And we've had a chance to talk about all the things that should've been said before."

Of his biological father, Harry Dixon, Terrance said, "He's my father, and, yes, he's done drugs and sold drugs and been in and out of jail. What can I say? I guess he's got his reasons, but with me, he was always there. If he had the time, he spent it with me. When he found out I'd been selling drugs that time—he found out a long time after it happened—he told me things that maybe people would say a good father shouldn't, but he said, 'Look, it's too dangerous out there for you to be doing this. If you want to be doing something, you come to me and we'll work something out. If you mess somebody up and they end up dead, they're going to shut the door.'

"He approached the problem in his own way. He was my father, what can I tell you? When he was home after he had been released from jail, you couldn't keep me away from him. If he was home, I was gonna see him, stay up under him."

Of his mother, Terrance said, "She was strong enough to be a fine lineman. She taught me how to play football. How many people can say they got to the college level and their mother taught them that?"

I thought of Ella Ross, four feet eleven, maybe one hundred pounds. Seeing the surprise on my face, Terrance said, "She taught me how to put my finger on the strings and throw. She taught me how to catch, you know, to watch the ball and catch it, things of that nature. You don't have to be big to know the fundamentals."

$$\bullet\ \bullet\ \bullet$$

I wondered if Terrance knew the real fundamentals his mother had taught and given him. I still did not know Terrance Brown when I left him that afternoon, but I knew what he had told me. His anecdotes, his observations, and his postures had created a picture of a youth who was, like many young men his age, conflicted about issues of power and identity. On the night of April 16, 1992, he was a young man who often settled disputes with violence. He loved his mother yet clearly yearned for the father he had not had, and he had not yet accepted the love Albert Ross extended. I wondered if Terrance Brown believed he deserved the promising future that had seemingly awaited him. Was there some part of him that saw himself not as Prime Time but as the son of a drug-dealing and -using father and the inheritor of a daunting level of sociological chaos and loss from the two families that had made him? Did Terrance Brown believe that despite the awards and the prizes, despite his mother's effort and the number of times she had beaten the odds, he was really a loser? Did that perhaps make it easier to endanger what he thought was not his by right to claim? Does a quick temper or choosing the wrong friends lead inevitably to robbery and murder? Legions of Black men in prison will tell you it can.

When I completed my interviews with Ella Ross and Terrance Brown, I talked with Michael about what I had discovered. A year had passed since Terrance's arrest. Michael had now had his own experience, albeit minor, with "the law." The average fourteen-year-old Black youth in Washington, DC, knows, as my son knew at the time of Terrance's arrest, of the reputation of the Prince Georges County police for being "tough on Black ass." If teens had not read about the numerous cases stretching back over two decades in which the Black community of Prince Georges County alleged excessive force or brutality, or in which Black suspects had been killed by the police under "unusual circumstances," then they had heard of these incidents from parents, relatives, or friends. Michael knew about the stories too. And because Terrance was initially placed in solitary confinement and there were rumors that Harry Mayo's damning testimony had been beaten out of him, Michael had at the beginning of Terrance's ordeal displayed the absolute conviction that Terrance was simply "set up."

I wondered how his views had changed in the intervening months. Was he still as certain as before that Terrance, like the man he had killed, was a victim?

So, one evening, I told Michael what I felt I knew, that Terrance, despite his outward confidence, was deeply troubled, and that, in a literal and figurative sense, he had been pulled by the competing values of the street and the straight life.

"Do you think he killed that guy on purpose?" Michael asked, stretching out on the sofa in my study.

"I don't know."

"If he hadn't had the gun," he said sadly, turning on his back to look at the ceiling. "He blew it."

"He said he was carrying the gun for protection," I said, deciding to play devil's advocate. "Remember when you were jumped by those boys near the subway and you were so angry you said you wished you had a gun, and if you did, you'd use it?"

"Yeah, but I was mad," he said, bolting upright in defense. "They shouldn't of jumped me. I didn't even know them."

"Maybe Terrance felt justified carrying a gun too."

"But he shot a cop. You know they'll never let him out. Not for killing a cop."

Terrance had ruefully predicted the same fate when I visited him.

"You know, when I was shoplifting that time, I knew it was wrong. But it was such a small thing, it didn't feel like a crime. Didn't you ever do something like that?"

Was I to tell him that when I was a college student, I routinely stole my required texts from the school bookstore? And that my friends and I had justified this act, calling it "liberation," not "theft," arguing that we were just reclaiming what "whitey" owed us anyway? I was never caught. So in the eyes of the law, I was innocent.

"Michael, it's your own soul, not mine, you're in charge of."

"I know you must've done something," he insisted, a mischievous gleam sparkling in his eyes, a smile crawling slowly across his face.

"You're my son, not my confessor. Now, come on and kiss me good-night so you can get ready for bed. You still aren't too big to do that."

• • •

JULY 10, 1993

Michael told me this evening that he has been having trouble sleeping at night as he thinks more and more about our trip. "Is it excitement or dread?" I asked. He said it was excitement.

JULY 13, 1993

*I talked today to Patrice Gaines, a friend and reporter for the **Washington Post**. She told me that last night her sixteen-year-old nephew was standing on a corner at Sixth and D Street SE with some friends talking when a young boy walked past them. A few minutes later, he walked back toward them and opened fire, shooting directly into their group. One young man was killed, one boy wounded; two others, including Patrice's nephew, were not hurt.*

Is the callousness of some of the young murderers any greater than our indifference to their fates before they buy and then use a gun? Once they are certified criminals, we lose sleep fearing they will be housed in jails in our neighborhoods or set free on bond to kill again. Many of these young men are deemed expendable, so why should they not commit acts so heinous that they slit the throat of our complacency? If the luckiest ones, like the students I saw at Howard a few months ago, can be Black any way they choose, for the rest, our contempt has freed them to destroy us and themselves with a cunning that leaves us awestruck. There is a war on Black men, one waged externally—an objective analysis of the statistics on who goes to jail for certain crimes and who doesn't reveals that. But there is the internal war Black men wage against each other as well. How do you fight on two fronts?

JULY 15, 1993

There was an article in the Post today concerning the shooting in which Patrice's nephew was involved. These were all just neighborhood boys, not drug dealers, standing on the corner on a summer night talking. One of the boys, Christopher Harvell, was a student of Joe's. He is a National Honor Society member who was class valedictorian at Dunbar this year and has been awarded a $100,000 scholarship from the Twenty- First Century Foundation to attend George Washington University, where he plans to study engineering. The dead youth, nineteen-year-old Henry Hank Lloyd, worked in a day-care center. Residents of the street say the youth who fired into the group feared they were rival drug dealers who planned to take over his corner.

JULY 17, 1993

Earlier in the week, the churches in the city declared a seventy-two-hour moratorium against violence. There was extensive news coverage of the marches, rallies, and prayer meetings. How do you gauge the success of an effort like this? What does it mean that there were only three homicides during the moratorium, one a seventeen-year-old witness to the killing of a Howard University security guard? The boy was shot twenty times in broad daylight, his body discovered in an alley behind Wiltberger Street, not far from our house.

Where do reason and reality intervene in all of this? I read an article this evening arguing that if all youths—white, Asian, Black, Hispanic, Native American, et al., urban, suburban, and rural—are compared proportionately, there are more Latino gangs than Black gangs, and that white youths are victims of all forms of violence more than Black youths. But statistics can't measure pain or transcribe fear. And frankly, more Latino gangs, more dead white youths, do not reduce the number of dead Black males. I am jealously possessive of every life. I refuse to compute an acceptable ratio of dead Black boys to compare to that of dead white boys. Statistics are beholden to their manipulators for meaning; they are slippery, fickle, ultimately untrustworthy bits of perception that the pundits worship like some essential cosmic truth. The language statistics speak is imposed, not intrinsic. So each time I read another story padded with numbers, graphs, charts, creating a logarithm of human destruction, I know that what we are living in America in these days is a story that is fantastic, extraliterary, mundane, unbelievable, and thus, all the numbers are completely false and all the numbers are completely true.

Clyde McElvene says he feels that if the kids being killed in the cities were overwhelmingly white, there would be a massive national response to stop the violence. But do the powers that be really care about kids, white or Black? I told Clyde that maybe if the children of congresspersons or senators or industrialists and business magnates were being assassinated in the streets, maybe then there would be the kind of response he envisions. But if those being killed were just regular working-class, poor, or even middle-class white kids, I didn't think the response would be much different. This country has yet to decide to guarantee the health, the education, the safety, and the economic viability of all children, so the horrid bloody drama unfolding on the streets of the Black community is no more than an unashamed echo of the society's lethal indifference to the fate of all our kids. The longer white America turns away from the sight of the body bags piling up on our streets, the more it ensures that even behind the actual and psychological barriers it has erected, the corpses of their own young will begin to pile up too.

JULY 19, 1993

I talked with Femi this morning. He said the atmosphere is still tense, but that while he can't guarantee anything, the worst of the demonstrations appear to be over. I keep trying to decide on an alternate time to make the trip. But there's no predicting that the situation will settle down anytime soon. I think I'm going to just act on faith and get on the plane.

JULY 25, 1993

Bade and his family and my friend Louise met us at Kennedy to await the boarding of the plane to Nigeria. We'll be okay. I've decided that.

SOON ONE MORNING

The Lagos to which Michael and I returned was a city that offered stark evidence of Nigeria's social and economic decline. The worldwide economic downturn had transformed a city that was often intractable yet infused with an irresistible vitality into a town that was prostrate, nearly defeated. No longer the "official" capital of the country, Lagos remains, however, the only place where the educated can make a decent living, the hungry can find food, and the ambitious are able to make it big.

Upon our arrival at Muritala Mohamad International Airport, Michael and I were Zprocessed through customs quickly. As we approached the baggage claim area, I spotted Femi and his older brother Jide waiting in the anterior section. Both men were clearly elated when they saw me and then Michael. Soldiers, some with rifles slung casually over their shoulders, patrolled the arrival section as we waited twenty minutes for our bags to appear on the carousel. I stood wondering at how easy this moment felt, a moment I had fought for and yearned for so long. My son's father stood fifty feet away from us, and the thought, even as soldiers stalked the halls around me, made me feel somehow safer than I had in many years.

Femi and Jide greeted us with hugs, and Jide, who possessed an innate, nearly indelible air of authority and a deep-throated, yet seductive laugh, marveled at Michael's height.

Michael stood shyly before Femi, fumbling for a way to approach his father. Femi was more reserved than Jide. As father and former husband, he had feelings at that moment which, I knew, were deeper, more complex.

Jide and Femi had driven to the airport in separate cars, so Femi packed our bags in his trunk and took Michael in his car while I rode with Jide. Formerly an executive with Phillips Electronics, Jide informed me that he had now retired and was working as a consultant. We talked about the political situation in the country. Jide praised the presidential election as the most free and fair in the country's history. But the national currency, the naira, was virtually worthless, he said; inflation was phenomenal, and when I began to talk about economic problems in the United States, Jide quieted me with a blustering laugh, scolding me with the words, "If America is asleep, Nigeria is dead."

Bade proudly told me that Lagos had expanded in size in the fourteen years since I'd left. Indeed, the roads into the city were, as I remembered them, jammed, movement paralyzed by the infamous Lagos "go slow." I saw along the highways a few gleaming imported Japanese Toyotas and Subarus and sturdy Mercedes-Benzes, which maneuvered the often crater-filled dirt side Hondas, canary-yellow ramshackle taxicabs, and bruised, battered, fifteen-to-twenty-seat passenger buses called danfos, each filled to capacity, all of them spewing forth noxious fumes and carbon monoxide that formed a dark toxic cloud that squatted over the length and breadth of the city.

The ranks of the roadside peddlers of cookies, milk, fruits, news-papers, and even sandals and live chickens had been swelled by grown men and women, sometimes whole families. No longer was this a job just for young children and teenagers. I saw for the first time scores of beggars. Lagos, whose inhabitants are perhaps the hardiest, hardest-working souls on the planet (and who live and thrive in the face of water shortages, constant electricity outages, a crumbling infrastructure, and an unresponsive, inept governmental bureaucracy), had always been nonetheless a city where even the poorest could find something to sell, something to do to survive. But the beggars I saw along the roads informed me conclusively how much things had changed. And I realized, less than an hour back in the Third World, that these young men standing beside these awful roads, breathing in poisonous fumes all day, chasing mobile potential customers, and dodging the world's worst drivers were "endangered" too, though not by violence but by poverty.

Femi had his own private real estate company, housed in a small suite of offices in a section of Lagos called Palm Grove. At Femi's offices, we found Jide's wife, Bisi, and their son, Akinyinka, await-ing our arrival. Bisi had acted as my unofficial Nigerian surrogate mother, aiding my adjustment to customs and family politics as well as nursing me through the loss of my first child and the healthy birth of Michael. So our reunion was affectionate and heartfelt. Bisi teased Michael, telling him that she had taught me how to change his diapers and making him sit beside her so that she could just place her arms around his shoulders while we all sat and talked. Her son, Akinyinka, had been seven when I left the country. He was now a college student, pleased to see Michael and me, but deferential, respectful of me, in a manner unique to children raised in more traditional societies. We sat in Femi's office remembering the past, updating one another on the present. Shade, Bisi and Jide's daugh-ter, was a student studying in London, and they showed me photos of her, a slender, beautifully coiffed and dressed young woman whose resemblance to her father was uncanny.

Soon Jide, Bisi, and Yinka departed, but before they left, Jide spoke for them all, I intuited, when he said to me as he looked again at Michael, tall, bright, and healthy, "Thank you for taking such good care of our son."

Michael wandered onto the balcony of Femi's office and stood talking with Leki, the brother of Femi's wife. Leki worked as Femi's messenger. Femi's secretary greeted me, saying, "Welcome, madam," with a slight bow, and I was thrust once again into the African caste system that I had never learned to accept fully. She was slight, attractive, her hair permed, her dress Western. Her deference to me was inspired by so much: I was a visitor, a guest, the former wife of her employer; I was an American, well educated, and a member of a higher "class" than she. Because of all this, from her perspective, real intimacy between us would be virtually impossible.

I watched Michael leaning on the iron banister with Leki, looking down on a street he had never seen before but watching it as though he had witnessed it every day of his life. And I heard the strains of the international language I soon learned connected young people around the world, making them a unique tribe of their own. The two stood talking animatedly about Michael Jordan, Michael Jackson, the rap group Naughty by Nature, Nike sneakers, Calvin Klein jeans.

Then Femi and I were alone in his office, and I wondered how to erase a decade of silence, hurt, and confusion. What did he feel at that moment? And because in our marriage it was always I who wanted to talk, to explain, to dissect and analyze, maybe too much, I took a deep breath and said simply, "Femi, I want to thank you for not dwelling on the past in your letters to me. I want to thank you for letting the past be just that."

"You were so afraid I would take Akintunde from you. You know I never meant those things I said."

"Femi, you only have to say the kinds of things you said once for them to be unforgettable, for them to hurt in a way that you think will never stop, for them to make you more afraid than you've been of anything before. You only have to say them once. You said them many more times than that."

"I never wanted to hurt you or Tunde. I never wanted to lose either of you."

"The letter I wrote you three years ago proves you didn't. Our presence here now does too."

And then we talked, about members of my family and close friends he remembered, and about his mother, now eighty-three, who had recovered from a long and deleterious bout with diabetes. Like everyone else in the country, he had been hit hard by the economic slump; still, he was building a house on the outskirts of Lagos and managing, he brooded gently, to keep "suffering and smiling," the Lagos motto for endurance in the face of adversity. In addition, he had been hospitalized for almost six months due to injuries suffered in a traffic accident, and he had lost money on some dubious investments. Femi was cynical, doubtful about the future of the country unless the President-elect was allowed to take office. As a businessman, he felt he could not leave Lagos, but the cost of living in the city, both financially and in terms of physical and emotional health, was staggering.

During our conversation, Michael entered the office and sat with us. As we talked, I savored this moment, the first time my son had seen me talking amicably with his father with no fear, no tension, in over a decade. It was a small moment, but one that contained the most valuable substance of all we would be given during this journey.

When we returned from lunch, Femi's wife, Ade, arrived, accompanied by Femi's four-year-old son, Akinyemi. Ade greeted me like an old friend, with an infectious smile for me and Michael. Our rapport was immediate as we talked about the resemblance between Michael and Akinyemi, the Nigeria Airways flight from New York, her job with the Education Ministry, mine at George Mason University. Yemi sat on the sofa sucking his thumb, quietly assessing Michael. He alternated a fascinated, studied watchfulness with the flickering beginnings of a smile as he warmed to his African-American brother. Michael led Yemi onto the balcony, where within moments Yemi was gleefully pummeling and punching Michael in a mock fight, yelling in his husky yet still childish voice, "I will beat you. I will beat you." English is the official language in Nigeria, the legacy of British colonialism; at his day-care center, Yemi learned English and Yoruba.

There came a moment when Ade, taking in the children, Femi, herself, and myself with a grand sweep of her arms, said, "I am glad we are happy together."

While Michael stayed with his father, I boarded with a cousin of one of Femi's oldest friends, Olu, who had been a kind of brother to me when Femi and I began dating. My host, Sola, was an administrator with the Lagos branch of an international bank. She made me feel entirely welcome in her home.

Michael spent most days with Femi at his office, watching him negotiate with clients or show various properties. One afternoon as

Michael and I sat on the balcony of Femi's office, an older, richly robed man approached the building. Michael said, with a shake of his head, "My father won't be happy to see that man. He says he's trying to cheat him, and he can't get away with that. I've watched my father work: He drives a hard bargain, he knows how to get what he wants."

Michael quickly became friends with a boy a year younger than himself who lived next door to Femi's office. My son greeted his father's friends with the required humble bow of the head and in awkward but sincere Yoruba, which I had taught him before our departure: "Ekuarro" ("Good morning"), "Odabo" ("Goodbye"). English was usually spoken in his presence, Yoruba if the conversation was confidential or private. When I, who had lived in Lagos for four years, complained of the relentless, endless snarl of traffic, the sporadic flow of electricity, Michael told me impatiently, "Mom, we're only gonna be here two weeks. You act like it's forever."

After witnessing Ade killing and plucking a live chicken for dinner one night, Michael became obsessed with the desire to kill a chicken on his own. One afternoon we went to the market with Ade. As we got out of the car, Ade winked at me and said in a serious, nearly ominous voice to Michael, "You want to kill a chicken, today you can kill a chicken. I will see to that."

The market was a series of twisting passageways lined with stalls selling anything that could be grown, made, or imported, legally or illegally. The market women, who had been at their posts since early morning, were as savvy as traders in oil or diamonds. As we passed the stalls, which curled in a seemingly endless labyrinth, the women called out, "Customer, customer." But Ade knew exactly where she was going, and we finally arrived at a spacious wooden stall filled from floor to ceiling with caged fowl. She told the owner in Yoruba that she wanted to buy a chicken. Then she grabbed Michael by the hand and together they inspected the caged birds. Michael pointed to several chickens. Ade and the owner haggled over size and price as Michael smiled at me, so excited he could barely stand still. I stood lagging behind them, amazed by this, to my mind, bloodthirsty display of aggression by my son. Was he merely going to assist Ade with dinner in this exercise, or was this desire symbolic of the serial killer lurking inside? I stood trying to remember that in two hours we would be feasting on whatever bird Michael chose and that then motivation wouldn't much matter.

Finally the bird was chosen and the owner's helper reached in and grabbed the squalling, healthy, white-feathered fowl by the neck. Ade paid for the bird. Michael was handed a machete and the bird was placed on the cement floor. Ade crouched on her knees holding the legs; the young helper held the head. Michael almost gleefully decapitated the chicken in two swift blows. The deed done, Michael danced proudly around the stall.

One evening a beggar ran up to the car window, his hand outstretched. The man hobbled on a makeshift cane fashioned from a stick and directed his gaze at Ade and then at me, but it was Michael who pleaded for coins to give him. Michael placed the coins in the man's hand with a solemnity and purpose that astonished me. Seeing this, Ade turned to me and said, "You took him away, but his soul remained here. He is an African."

Nigeria was in the throes of a religious boom. One day as Ade and I talked about the hundreds of churches that had sprung up all over Lagos, she told me, "Times are so hard now, and people feel, if you can't have bread, at least you can have God." Billboards lined the major and minor roads; fliers and posters seemingly filled every inch of public space advertising congregations like the Faith Family

Church, the poster illustrated with a drawing of a contented family gazing heavenward. Evangelists aired televised services.

The evening news was tightly controlled by the military government, and each evening at Sola's, I watched the melodramatic, tragic accounts, which were really undisguised propaganda urging the country to remain calm, not to take to the streets once again. I sat depressed and uncertain each evening, watching footage of delegations of politicians, from all the political parties and from around the country, meeting with Babangida, who vainly attempted to appear to be a statesman rather than a thief. Numerous newspapers and magazines had been seized and shut down, their editors and journalists thrown in jail for any act or word deemed critical of the government. Femi refused to read The Daily Times, now considered a mere mouthpiece for the military government that refused to step down. In Femi's office each afternoon, the talk was as much of the fate of the country as of business.

One afternoon, Michael, Yemi, Yinka, and I went on an excursion to Lekke Beach, located on Victoria Island, an exclusive preserve where diplomats, wealthy foreigners, and many affluent Nigerian businessmen owned spacious apartments and homes.

Femi's driver took us into the city. The traffic in Lagos is a hydra-headed monster, and even in the midst of a gasoline shortage in this oil-producing country that had motorists waiting hours in line for petrol and had decreased the number of cars on the roads, the traffic remained a test of ingenuity, strength, and will. There were no driving schools in Lagos, and so on the roads and behind the wheel, improvisation most often reigned. On the bridge leading to Lagos Island, the commercial heart of the city, we passed an accident. The two drivers, one a burly danfo driver whose facial tribal marks unfurled like foliage on his cheeks, and the other a well-dressed driver of an Acura Legend whose suit I had seen in the window of Hugo Boss in Washington's fashionable Georgetown shopping district, stood raining curses upon one another. The front of the Legend was dented, and the owner gazed at the car as if assessing the broken body of a family member. The two men were, as we snaked by them, in the midst of a furious bout of posturing, one that allowed them to approach one another within a few feet, make a series of insulting, metaphorically lethal gestures with arms and hands, and curse and slander one another, all while being reined in by the crowd that had gathered around them.

I knew that someone in the crowd would mediate a face-saving way for each man to leave the scene with some measure of dignity intact. A foul curse upon one's house or family was as lethal as these altercations got. The thought that a private citizen would reach into a car trunk or beneath a car seat and pull out a gun to close the matter was inconceivable.

In the back seat, as we neared the beach, Michael and Yinka sat discussing the film *Boyz N the Hood*, which Yinka had seen on video. (Nearly every middle-class home I had entered since our arrival had a VCR.) Despite the seven-year age difference, the two talked animatedly and shared numerous interests. Listening to them, I remembered Michael's question, "What would I be like if I had grown up in Nigeria?" Bisi and I had talked about our sons. When Yinka was fourteen, she sent him to a private boarding school in Ondo State for reasons similar to those that had made me choose Westtown as an option and opportunity for Michael. "Oh, he was silly, and immature, playful. I felt he really needed to be away from us," she explained with a laugh. "By the time he graduated, you know, they had straightened him out."

But I knew that my son, had he come of age in Nigeria, would have been less individualistic, more conscious of and influenced by family, community, tribe. I knew, too, that he would have taken his racial identity for granted as a reality, neither positive nor negative, in a way that was impossible in the highly charged, insidiously racial atmosphere of America.

At twenty-two, Yinka had only one more year of undergraduate studies to complete before graduating. But for the past three years, the military government had closed colleges and universities throughout the country in labor disputes with faculty over pay, and many felt it had been done to neutralize the political influence of students, often the first to demonstrate and rally against government policy.

As Shade was her father's daughter, Yinka was his mother's son, possessing her long, angular, open face even while he had his father's height. When we arrived at the beach, Michael and Yinka swam for several hours while Yemi and I collected seashells. Then, over a lunch of barbecued meat, I asked Yinka about his studies at the University of Lagos, where I had once taught. Three months before our arrival, the government had closed the university, effectively canceling the remainder of the term. Yinka was an English major but said that ultimately he wanted to study law or international relations at the graduate level. When I asked him what I had asked Marc, if there was anything that he feared when he thought about the future, he said, "I'm afraid I won't be able to be someone who can raise and take care of a family, someone whom others can depend on, not someone depending on anyone else." The stagnant economy had turned the search for employment Yinka had launched since the university shutdown into a futile, cruel joke.

More than anything, he told me, he longed for money and a passport to go to England to join his sister Shade. "At least there, the universities wouldn't be closed, I could finish my education, get my degree."

As I listened to the sincerity and frustration in my young relative's voice, I thought of the violent climate of racial intolerance then infecting England and so much of Europe, which had made cities like London, Paris, and Berlin, once hallowed in the minds of former colonials, dangerous places for "colored" men and women. And even more unjust, I felt, was that twenty years after Jide had journeyed abroad to study, idealistically hoping to return and build a viable nation, Nigeria could neither absorb his son's considerable talents in the job market nor guarantee him a seat in the university. Yinka's plight mirrored the bitter, unfinished legacy my generation had bequeathed our sons and daughters in the generation after the civil rights struggle. I was learning every day how slippery and relative concepts like "safety" or "progress" could be in these days of global interdependence, with the Third World tottering beneath the weight of a "new world order" more exploitative, racist, and dangerous than the old one. Everywhere I looked, my people were plugging holes in the same rickety boat.

• • •

How to determine the quality and quantity of affection and trust that Michael and Femi shared, found, built? I watched Femi with Yemi, who, at four, had a Herculean temper, yet who was engaging and curious and saw a parent at once indulgent and firm. What kind of father would he have been to Michael? I vaguely recalled that in the first year of Michael's life, he was a proud father, protective of his son, unwilling to deny him anything. I spent two evenings with Femi and Ade and saw that the initial awkwardness between Femi and Michael has dissolved—without me. Already Michael had learned

Saving Our Sons

how far he could go in negotiating favorable terms for his requests, and Femi attempted to balance the imposition of boundaries and limits with indulgence, perhaps to make up for all the lost time. They watched televised soccer together, played marathon games of Monopoly. A thousand small verbal exchanges, facial expressions, mundane conversations, jokes, irritations, moments of laughter, political debates, untruths, and inquisitions created something between them that Michael could not, when I asked him, explain, but only possess.

I had awaited this journey with greater anticipation, I felt, than even Michael, and so I was eager in the midst of it to gain a sense of what was transpiring between father and son, how they found the way, each day, to one another. When I asked Michael one afternoon how he and Femi were getting along, he told me, "You know, my father doesn't really talk a lot. He asks the kind of questions you ask somebody you don't know."

"That's to be expected."

"He asks what I like to do, what I want to study in college, what I'd like to be when I grow up."

"Do you feel distant from him?"

"Not distant, but I feel closer to Yemi and Yinka."

"He loves you. I hope you can see that, even though it's hard for him to express it."

As we talked, I thought of the way Femi possessively threw his arm around Michael when they sat in the back seat of the car together. I knew that displays of affection were difficult for him. That arm casually slung over our son's shoulder, and the look on Femi's face that articulated a subtle, hard-won contentment, reveling quietly in the moment, spoke what Michael was too young to hear or understand.

And Michael had not been privy to my conversation with Femi in which he told me, "Things are terrible in the country right now. But by the time Akintunde is ready for college, he could come here for a year or so and it wouldn't be as expensive as in the States." I thought of the closed university campuses but also of the young woman we had met at Kennedy Airport the evening of our departure. Her father was Yoruba and her mother was African American. She was twenty years old and told us that after her parents divorced when she was five, she remained in Nigeria with her father for several years, then came to the United States to live with her mother. With her cornrowed hair, her bubbly charm, and the ease with which she spoke Yoruba, the young woman was impressive. She lived a transatlantic life, shuttling between Nigeria and the United States easily, and she had studied for a time at the University of Lagos before it was closed by the government. I looked at the young woman and hoped Michael would one day fit as easily as she in both the homes he could legitimately claim.

And there was often a softness, a gentleness, in Femi's voice as he spoke to Michael. His pride was evident when he introduced him to friends or associates, who were amazed at Michael's height and how much he resembled Femi. "This is my son, who lives in America with his mother," he'd say.

There was the list Michael was compiling of items to bring to Nigeria to sell when he came back to visit again—tapes, clothing, watches. He asked me to help him make purchases for such a trip. Femi had promised to help him sell whatever he brought. This entrepreneurial zeal was Femi's imprint, not mine.

Michael had returned to Nigeria to claim his status as "older son" in Femi's house. He was part oyingbo, "foreigner," but he was also blood and the firstborn male child. And so Femi indulged him, scolded him, but gently, when required, and had Ade prepare fried chicken, french fries, salad, and other American dishes to accommodate Michael's palate. Femi did all this not because Michael was a guest but because he was his boy-child.

And so I told Michael, "It will take time to build the closeness. I just wanted you to know your father and that he is here for you."

"I'm glad we came. And I want to come back. I'm glad I've seen my father. I have friends who never did. Their dads died when they were real young, or they walked out on the family. At least I got to see my father and know who he is."

Femi and Michael were separated as much by the passage of time as by culture. For the intense conversations that Michael often shared with Joe, during which they discussed sports and politics and life almost as equals, were absent in Nigeria. Michael's opinion was unsought by his father or the Ajayi clan, even while they loved him and celebrated his return. The lines of demarcation between parent and child were bolder in this society that as stranger and inheritor my son sought to claim.

• • •

Several days before our departure, Femi, Jide, Michael, and I drove to Femi's hometown, Ado Ekiti, to visit his mother. We arrived in the town near dusk after a five-hour drive from Lagos. Our first stop was at a large, many-roomed house owned by Jide and used by family members visiting Ado Ekiti, for Femi's mother had little space in her house for visitors.

Femi's mother was Michael's only living grandparent. She was the only person in whose face he could see what elements of biology and character spawned one of his parents. She was the only living thread my son had to the genesis of what and who created him.

There was electricity in the town now and the major road leading into Ado Ekiti was paved. But there had been no water running through the town's pipes for the past four days, and driving in the early evening dusk to Femi's mother's house, we passed young girls and boys, men and women, carrying buckets of water retrieved from the town's main pump. Progress had arrived, I was told, but Ado Ekiti remained a town mostly of goats, old people, and small children. Years before, when I had visited Femi's mother for the first time, a goat was slaughtered in celebration. But inflation had made such a feast impossible to consider for Michael's return, and we stopped several times during the drive to buy yams, fruit, and bread for Femi's mother, for hunger had returned to many parts of the country outside the large cities.

"Mama," as I had always called Femi's mother, stood in her tiny parlor awaiting our arrival. Despite her battle with diabetes, the only change was the color of her cornrowed hair, now almost solidly white. One of eight wives, a devout Christian who honored both the Western God and her traditional tribal beliefs, she urged Femi and Jide to take only one wife. Once she told me that now that I was an Ajayi, she finally had a daughter. I laughed, suspecting that she had told Bisi, Jide's wife, this as well. But that did not matter, for her loyalty was inclusive and resilient. She was the only person whom Femi truly feared and respected, the only person in the family whose will he would, in moments of anger, submit to without question.

The tiny brown eyes embedded in her amazingly unlined face were luminous when she spotted Michael striding into the room behind

Femi. She clapped her hands, gazed skyward, and mouthed a prayer in Yoruba, thanking God for our return. As required, Michael, all five feet eight of him, prostrated himself before his grandmother as a sign of respect, and she smiled broadly in satisfaction and pleasure. My son had, according to his father's tradition, merely given the woman to whom he in some measure owed his life a small part of her due.

Mama shared her house with almost a dozen people who rented rooms from her. And so, small children with huge searching eyes and distended bellies; young girls, giggling and surprised by the sight of my son, tall, wearing braces, speaking a language they only partially understood; and young women who helped care for Mama and who had been told that her grandson was coming from America—all stood on the edges of the room, witnesses to our reunion.

Femi translated for me, for his mother spoke no English. Michael gave her the strand of pearls we brought as a token, and, as she placed them around her neck, he told a young woman to bring her a mirror. Satisfied with what she saw in the mirror, she then paraded around the small room cocking her head in a merry display, to the delight of all gathered. I had given Femi three hundred dollars for his mother, which he had sent to her via a friend days before our arrival, and she thanked me for the money.

Once again she launched into prayer, this time urging us all onto our knees. After the prayer, she gazed at me with a mischievous yet determined look in her eye and asked through Femi if I would stay this time. I told her that I had a husband back in the States to whom I must return. She accepted my answer but assured me that I remained her daughter nonetheless.

As Femi and his mother talked, through the small window I heard a small radio perched between two men sitting outside, and on it the sound of a French radio station. Femi told me that among the people who now lived with his mother were immigrants from Mali who had fled that country because of the drought.

Michael sat in our midst, fidgeting, bored. After a while, he asked if he could go outside to sit on the front porch. Femi and I said that he could.

As Femi and I prepared to return to the guest house, we went outside to find Michael in animated conversation with several young women and men. In the darkness, Michael sat on the small cement stoop, encircled by a group of young girls and women, who sat rapt, listening to him talk. Femi laughed and told me that he was certain that because of Michael's accent, those gathered understood perhaps only half of what he said. But clearly they were enthralled by his height, his strong, aggressive presence, and the way he used space and his body.

"Tomorrow they will brag that they met an oyingbo," Femi said.

Michael begged to stay there for the night. "At least there's someone here to talk to," he explained. "Back there it's just you adults."

The next morning, when we drove back to Mama's house to get Michael, he told us that he had slept with his grandmother because there was no extra bed. I recalled that on my first visit I had shared a bed with Mama too, while Femi slept in his father's house. My rest had been calm and unperturbed. Michael said mosquitoes kept him awake all night. When I asked how he communicated with Mama, Michael shrugged, saying simply, "We figured it out." Then I took pictures of Femi, Mama, and Michael together, gave small monetary tokens to several elders who lived nearby, and with hugs and promises, we said goodbye.

On the way out of the town, Femi showed Michael several plots of land that he had inherited on his father's death, land formerly used as part of his father's rubber plantation.

"I'm going to retire here," he said.

"You'll never retire," I teased him. "You'll never leave Lagos."

"Yes I will."

"I want to live to see it."

"So do I." He smiled.

"Because this land is mine, it's also yours," Femi told Michael, staring at him in the rearview mirror. "I will see to that."

I settled back in my seat in the front watching Ado Ekiti pass by and thought that maybe as much as Michael had come back to find his father, he had returned as well to claim another "place" that could be his. He had found a father, cousins, aunts, uncles—and land, untilled, lying fallow, but his one day, on which he could make something grow.

• • •

Shortly after our return from Nigeria, we moved to Mitchellville, Maryland. In mid-September, Michael entered Westtown. I learned quite soon that Michael had not merely been "sent away" to school but had become part of an academic, cultural, and social community that would have potentially enormous impact on him.

I missed him intensely the first several weeks, but gradually came to appreciate the peace of mind that came with knowing he was in a safe environment. The school year in Washington had opened on a violent note when, on the second day of classes, a junior high school student sprayed random gunfire into a group of other students walking to a bus stop.

At Westtown, Michael, always socially adept, quickly made friends. But his mid-term grades the first semester were dismal. And shortly after Thanksgiving, I received a call from the school psychologist, who told me several of Michael's teachers had begun to suspect that his poor performance was an indication of attention deficit disorder. In response, she had conducted a series of tests with Michael that indicated he might indeed suffer from ADD, but a more formal diagnosis was still needed. The school psychologist phoned one day before I had planned to restart the diagnostic process at the National Institutes of Health with a call to Dr. Zametkin.

By the time he came home for Christmas, Michael knew that his difficulties in consistently achieving up to his potential might be neurologically based. But he was angry and confused, and thought that the results of the tests the school psychologist had given him meant he was retarded. A few days before Christmas, Dr. Peter Jensen, an associate of Dr. Zametkin's at NIH, talked at length with Michael and with Joe and me about Michael's problems in paying attention and completing tasks both at home and at school. He also assessed the test results from Westtown and the reports of Michael's teachers. Dr. Jensen diagnosed Michael as suffering from ADD. Because Michael was not hyperactive, it had been very difficult to recognize the signs of ADD earlier. Dr. Jensen told us that like many of those with the disorder, Michael was very bright and articulate and could focus intensely on subjects that interested him. His attention span was fractured, however, when it came to *assigned* tasks.

On Christmas Eve, I took Michael to see Audrey Chapman, for I was worried about his continuing inability to accept the fact that he had a learning difference and about his fear that it meant he was mentally handicapped. Michael talked with Chapman in detail about his fears, his anxieties, his questions. Perhaps because he had confided in her before, after talking with him for an hour, she was able to convince him to work with the staff at Westtown, with his doctor, and with Joe and me to develop a treatment strategy.

From the sessions with Dr. Jensen and Audrey Chapman, I learned for the first time that Michael often simply "phased out" in the middle of classroom lectures, that he would frequently begin a project and simply be unable to continue to focus. Michael had never told me any of this. He did not know how.

I felt tremendous relief, for I felt that I finally knew why there had been such a wide and continuing gap between Michael's potential and his achievement. The treatment strategy consisted of medication, as well as special tutoring tailored to his learning style and designed to help him develop techniques that would enable him to stay on task and become more organized. I had been told by the school psychologist that there were numerous students at Westtown who had ADD and who performed well academically.

In my need to help Michael cope with the implications of the diagnosis, I read several books on attention deficit disorder. One book, written by a respected educational psychologist, asserted that nearly all American schoolchildren suffered unprecedented levels of inattention, lack of focus, and poor concentration. The pervasive influence of television and video games and the radical changes in family cohesion and parenting styles had produced, this author argued, a generation of youngsters whose thought patterns were fuzzy and incomplete and who had difficulty digesting any idea that couldn't be grasped in thirty seconds.

But the more I read about ADD, the more conflicting seemed the evidence of its prevalence. The diagnostic process had relied heavily on anecdotal summaries from Michael, his teachers, and Joe and me. Why, I began to wonder, were middle- and upper-class children disproportionately diagnosed as having learning disabilities? Did the goal-oriented, achievement-conscious values of upscale families encourage labeling of any child who failed early on to achieve high grades? The evidence seemed to support this conclusion. Why was it so frequently recommended that boys essentially be medicated in the classroom? A pediatrician friend warned me, explaining, "ADD has become the fashionable diagnosis. It's overdiagnosed and is used to explain a myriad of connected and disconnected behavior and learning problems."

After months of reading, researching, and talking with parents whose children had been diagnosed with various learning differences, I concluded that I simply did not know for sure whether Michael suffered from ADD—that really, nobody knew.

I did know that, at sixteen, my son had a pattern of problems in sustaining focus and attention academically. In public school, Michael had typically played his way through the first half of the year, and then, fearing summer school or failure, had made average to good grades in the final semester. Did Michael have ADD, or was he just lazy? Did he require intense pressure to perform well at tasks he wasn't drawn to? Even his admission that he "phased out" in class was not necessarily definitive, at least not to me. Was he unable to be attentive, or was he easily distracted? Did he choose not to concentrate? I began to wonder if maybe my son's public school teachers' conclusion that "he just hasn't learned to buckle down," or their conjecture that "he'll grow out of it," might not be just as valid as Dr. Jensen telling Joe and me that, with the passage of adolescence, the symptoms of ADD subside in some children and they can learn to compensate for their learning problems without the use of drugs.

By the end of the first year at Westtown, Michael had raised his grades, although they remained marginal. He remained sporadically disorganized and often inconsistent in his approach to studying, but he spoke more often than in the past of really wanting to do well academically. He began talking about college and careers he was considering. Michael was growing up, struggling to meet the expectations of parents and teachers, as well as suddenly new expectations of himself, which he had perhaps been afraid to impose before. The academic rigors of Westtown had challenged him, and he admitted more than once that he felt "special" as a member of the Westtown community.

During this first year, Michael had battled with fears that he was academically out of his league, had read Zora Neale Hurston's *Their Eyes Were Watching God*, had shone in his theater class, had learned to grasp equations in algebra, had been a member of the basketball and baseball teams, had run for the post of prefect on his floor, and had counted as one of his best friends at the school a young man from Malaysia. I had stayed in touch regularly with his advisors and counselors, his tutor and teachers, attempting to monitor his progress while not making him feel burdened by my intrusions. Michael was literally surrounded by a human safety net of adults, all of whom worked with and came to know him intimately, and who like me pushed and encouraged him to do nothing less than his best.

I now felt ready to work with him more on consciously building his confidence and self-esteem, modifying his behavioral patterns and his attitude toward responsibility, and relying a little less on the medication. The diagnostic process had given me crucial information about my son that I might not have discovered any other way. And using this information, I was learning what systems of rewards and punishments, what types of motivation and encouragement, worked best with Michael. As his parent, it was my responsibility to combine a close reading of the child I still knew better than any doctor with a critical assessment of the treatment prescribed for whatever medical problems he was deemed to possess. Because Michael tended in his behavior often to take shortcuts, I felt that reliance on medication transmitted exactly the opposite message a child with his inclinations should receive.

In one year, my son had been reunited with his father, had left home to attend boarding school, and had had thrust upon him an unsettling, unfamiliar assessment of his abilities. Michael was still learning how emotionally strong he could be. He remained, then, a child, an adolescent, stumbling yet guided by the map made by those who loved him toward an adulthood he could not fathom but only fiercely desire.

I do not know what choices my son will make, what type of life he will live, what he will choose to believe, how he will use his talents. I do know that he was, and is, loved. I know that he has seen those who cared about him reach always for the highest and brightest star. I only wish for Michael his own galaxy and the determination to reach for it himself.

Saving Our Sons

EPILOGUE

Every sentence is a search for truth. Each paragraph is a window; each page, an open door. I wrote about sons because at this moment there is no subject more necessary to confront, more imperative to imagine. Until I wrote about our sons, I could not speak or think or dream of anything else.

The specter of death, real, unexpected, and cruel, has filled these pages. Death, like some medieval plague, is now with us. And if we love our sons and our daughters and ourselves, we must speak death's name, step up to it, challenge it, fight it collectively and one-on-one.

But an insatiable desire for, and commitment to, life has fueled these words. We bury and mourn the sons who are dead. What will we do to cherish and save the ones who live?

If the daily transgressions against safety, sanity, and well-being that prevail in pockets of the Black community were committed against us by members of any other race, these acts would be labeled terrorism. How else to describe a group of boys on a street corner forcing a young man at gunpoint to first hand over his coat and then strip naked? Clothes were stolen, but dignity was appropriated as well. Standing outside my husband's school at dusk that evening, perhaps hoping as he disrobed that a police car might happen by, the young man probably mumbled what he thought would be his last prayer ever. For he had grown up in the neighborhood, was on his way to an after-school job. He knew that the slightest glimmer of insolence, rebellion, or anger reflected in his voice or eyes could inspire a finger to press the trigger.

In the opening pages, I metaphorically claimed both the young man standing naked on a nighttime street corner and the boys who sped off with his clothes as my sons. What else was I to do? So I urge us to tell our sons every day, over dinner, in the bathroom, in school, on the basketball court, on the phone, during the commercial break, in Sunday school, before they go to bed, when they get up, when they head off to college, when they come home, when we visit them in jail, when we attend their weddings, when we mourn at the funerals of their friends: You have a choice, you are responsible for what you do, and your community will hold you accountable. Racism will never change that. Long after our eyes glaze over and our ears grow numb watching and listening to the TV roundtable discussions that seek to address our fate, we can still keep our sons awake and perhaps alive if we teach them that the first line of defense against racism is to mold themselves into disciplined, self-respecting refutations of its ability to destroy our souls or ourselves. This is not a platitude. And telling our sons they can make a choice and not have life merely happen to them does not render the choices always palatable or benign.

Of course, in the most ultimate, far-reaching sense, it is only the dismantling of institutional racism that will guarantee the lives of our sons and all our children. All the most objective and uniformly respected studies have found, year after year, that my son, prep school-educated and world-traveled, will nevertheless be discriminated against in every endeavor of his life, from hailing a taxi to applying for a job or a mortgage to buying a car. Michael, like all of America's Black sons, pays a "Black tax" on his existence every day of his life. I am anguished and angry confronting that reality. Our sons are too.

The lives and legacy of African Americans have been progressive and valuable beyond measure simply because each generation has fashioned a way to resist the pernicious hold of racism on our lives. My son's generation is the first that may be destroyed before it can marshal its forces against the enemy arrayed at the border. The battle this time is even bloodier, the lines more deeply drawn.

And yet this examination of my life and my son's life has revealed answers embedded in the minutiae of my struggle to make it through each day, answers I fashioned unknowingly, with fingers crossed in the dark, afraid I'd never see the light: answers that I found because I was more afraid not to seek them out than I was of what they might be.

African-American women must forgive the real and imagined crimes of their sons' fathers. We must resist the urge to visit upon all the men in our lives the bitterness and pain planted by incompetent fathers or disappointing lovers. Forgiving Michael's father was the most important, difficult action I have taken in my role as mother. There is nothing else that I have done for my son that approaches that step in importance. Forgiving my son's father did not transform my ex-husband, but it did allow Michael to see the best in me, and it paved a path for him to cross to reach the man who gave him life. Our sons need their fathers, even when they are absent; they need to know who they are so that they can confirm their own identity. The generations-old backlog of anger that African-American men and women hoard, revisit, and, with a genius that is frightening, unleash upon one another becomes a script that our sons and our daughters memorize, practicing its lethal intent and perfecting it in their own lives.

We Black women must forgive Black men for not protecting us against slavery, racism, white men, our confusion, their doubts. And Black men must forgive Black women for our own sometimes dubious choices, divided loyalties, and lack of belief in their possibilities. Only when our sons and our daughters know that forgiveness is real, existent, and that those who love them practice it, can they form bonds as men and women that really can save and change our community.

In the absence of traditional family structures, we can and must recreate the meaning of family. That was formerly one particular genius of African Americans. Every Black church in America should adopt and become responsible for the sons of its racial community as well as the sons of its congregation.

There was a transcendent moment in our history when we faced bulldogs, water cannons, jail cells, firebombs, assassinations, and sacrifice so that our children could be full citizens. What will we do so that they can live? We have faced guns before. In the past they were aimed at us by mobs cloaked in white sheets, but never held on us by our own sons. Do we now fear our children more than we feared racists? Did we want to integrate more than we now want to save ourselves from extinction?

We know what is required, a moral and ethical transformation that will make us both bold and compassionate, intuitive and strategic, demanding and forgiving. We created and became our best selves in the "struggle for freedom." Why do we resist the same call to deliver our young? The chaos that reigns in pockets of the Black community today is as arbitrary, complicated, and fearsome as the brutality of the undeclared guerrilla war that Southerners unleashed to preserve segregation.

We know how to win moral and material skirmishes, how to create an army of domestic workers, college students, janitors, and preachers. We know how to march and shame a nation. Our failure to push ourselves past the net of the conventional, the safe, shames us now. The present challenge descends directly from the partial answers, the unfinished business, that Black and white America left behind in a rush toward self-congratulation. Paralyzed by debate, indifferent, factionalized, unable to caucus unless the cameras wait outside the door, we watch as our sons meanwhile embrace destruction. We will not place ourselves between them and the madness because we don't love them enough to insist, to demand, to require that they live.

NOVEMBER 10, 1993

Joe came home from school today and handed me the following note which he had written during his lunch break:

Marita, I feel the need to write and communicate with God. People like you grab your pen and write out your problems or write through them. But today I was faced with something I had feared for some time. During the 1985–86 school year, I met a teacher who had lost one of her students to violence. Two Black males took the student's boom box and blew him away. I felt so sorry for that teacher that I prayed for the child, for his parents, and for the teacher. In the years since then, I have prayed as well for students, former students, just that they would be safe, that they would survive. But today it happened, what I had been afraid of. I wonder. Only God knows. A student in my homeroom has contracted AIDS. Do we have to literally step over our children's dead bodies? When will it end?

Love, Joe.

Marc decided a year after taking my class at Antioch that he indeed did want to pursue a career as a writer. He won an honorable mention in a national competition for African-American college writers, the Zora Neale Hurston/Richard Wright Award. His story "Mercury" was awarded third place out of forty-seven submissions from all over the country. Marc decided to study creative writing at the graduate level after he graduated from Antioch. Marc is the author of the novel *The Year of the Rat*, which won the American Book Award, and the novel *Messiahs*. He teaches creative writing at the University of Pennsylvania.

Terrance Brown took college courses offered at the Lorton Correctional Complex by Coppin State College and made the dean's list and the honor roll. His name was submitted to the National Dean's List directory for inclusion in the 1994–95 edition. Terrance died while incarcerated.

Michael entered the eleventh grade at Westtown and for the first time in years began the academic year confident and achieving good grades. He admitted that in his first year at Westtown he was girl crazy and had not studied. At sixteen, going on seventeen, he was suddenly obsessed with making good grades and getting into a good college. Today, Michael is a social media influencer. His wife is a professor of political science and they have a daughter.

THE DEAD CALL US TO REMEMBER

Below are some of the men who have died violently in Washington, DC, since 1988. They were killed during arguments, robberies, drug deals, while at play, sitting in cars, standing on corners, in their homes, walking home from work, in alleys, and on playgrounds. They were thirteen, forty-two, seventy-four, and their deaths were caused by knife stabs, beatings, and gunshots. Some were shot as they sat in cars, others were shot from passing cars. They died at midnight, in the middle of the day. They were barbers, mechanics, owners of their own businesses, rap musicians, white-collar workers, gang members and schoolboys and fathers and husbands and sons.

Kevin Darnell

Louis W. Gelman

Donnie Michaels

Christophe Jones

Ernest P. McQueen

Floyd Payne

Terrance Sealey

Joseph T. Sams

Michael R. Robinson

Linden S. Ault

Thomas Brown, Jr.

Eric N. Butler

Bob Gerald Trever

Jamie Banker

Raymond Campbell

Raymond C. Davidson

Eugene M. Artis

Demitrius Coleman

David Williams

Maurice W. Crutchfield

William C. Johnson

William A. Best

Frederick Glenn

Julian Timberlake

Darnell Wells

Habib Mathis

Anthony F. Bailey

Derrick W. Bell

Richard Lewis Clark

Cecil R. Curry

Carlton Earl Dickens

Derrick Chase

Gary Hickman

Leonard Allen Morrison

Cedric M. Johnson III

Jimmy Blade

Anthony E. Wright

Wesley S. Gorham

James A. Mingo

Darryl Johnson

Willard E. Jones

Larry A. Rawles

Thomas W. Moore

Robert Lee Hill

Anthony L. Slappy

Paul A. Frazier

Norman R. Oakcrum

Julio Perryman

Reginald K. Peters

William Craig Haley

Norman Brown

Mawu Robinson

Cassius C. Keys

Anthony T. Tate

Vernon A. Mitchell

Steven West

Michael Olds

Robert E. Lewis

Keith Mayo

Kenneth Jones

Kevin A. Clements

Christopher Conley

Lawrence Monroe

Franklin Smith

Lonnie O. Hutchinson

Warren Harris

Ronald K. Thompson

Lee Oliver Williams

Donald Bolton

Zachery J. Ray

Julius Robinson

Eddie Nell Martin

Tachious J. Owens

Reginald Lewis

Reginald Duckett

James Harris Brooks

Warren Morgan

Stanley McCrae

Cory Hines

Steven L. Parker

Emory Lewis Trawick

Lonnie Hart, Jr.

Albert Thomas

Reginald Walker

Steven Maxwell

Alvin Winstock

Daryl W. Murchison

David Lewis Hodge

Anthony Paul Hestop

Melvin Douglas Brown

Michael McCurdy

Samuel A. Mack

Kevin Eans

William A. Wilson

Larry McCaspling

Wade Malone

Johnnie Lee Green

Victor O. Tatum

Albert E. Webb

Bobby Workman

Charles Brandon, Jr.

Kevin A. Henson

Edward D. Pelham

Anthony Settlers

Yusef "Yukie" Belton

William Edward Howard

Warren Jackson

An unidentified man

Adolph Martino

Hector Colon

Bruce Lee Parks

Al Johnson

David Kevin Lee

Shonie Clatterbuck

Gregory Jones

David Julien

Donald Johnson

Marx V. Brown

Alonzo D. Allen

David A. Stamper, Jr.

Stephan P. Smith

Ernest E. Young

Martin Freeman

Neil Abbie Thompson

Michael Graham

Gary Wayne Pfleger

Donnell P. Winley

Wayne Huff

Darren Alston

Dwight D. George

RESOURCE GUIDE FOR PARENTS AND CAREGIVERS

WHY THIS RESOURCE GUIDE?

There is an African proverb that says a child who does not feel the warmth of his village will burn it to the ground to feel the warmth of the fire. As a single mother raising a Black son, Marita Golden learned very quickly that for her son to reach maturity, she would need help from the community. When community was not available to her, she and others built their own group to meet and discuss what they were going through and to lean on each other for support. Tracking down sources of support took effort and time, and information was not always readily available.

It is our hope that this resource guide will help save you some legwork and provide you with information you can use as you raise or mentor Black boys in your own life. Our goal is to provide a resource guide that will stand the test of time and offer you a comprehensive list of places you can go to seek help and advice. While there is a focus on providing support for Black men and boys, several of these resources can be helpful to Black women and girls, as well as parents of Black children who are not Black themselves.

We are hopeful that the information provided here will be a resource you can use as a guide to avoid feeling helpless and isolated, and to provide Black males with the services and support they need.

Marita Golden, author of *Saving Our Sons*
MJ Fievre, author of *Raising Confident Black Kids*

EMERGENCY HELPLINE

The problem of suicide among Black males is an increasing matter of urgency. A 2018 study in *Scientific American* reported that Black children between the ages of five and twelve are twice as likely to die by suicide as white children of the same age group. Suicide rates for Black boys are 2.5 times the rate of Black girls, and boys who attempt suicide are more likely to die in the attempt because they tend to use more deadly methods than girls and often act on impulse.[1] Hotlines provide 24-hour support with trained counselors who can talk you (or an individual with suicidal thoughts) through a crisis. It is urgent that you reach out if someone you know is talking about suicide. This is often a call for help that can prevent tragedy.

- **Suicide Prevention Lifeline:** 1(800)273-TALK (8255) or 1-800-SUI-CIDE (routes to the same hotline). The Suicide Prevention Lifeline provides 24-hour assistance to those in crisis or contemplating suicide and to their loved ones, as well

1   https://www.kqed.org/news/11501627/data-exclusive-75-percent-of-black-california-boys-dont-meet-state-reading-standards

as a live online chat function with trained counselors on their website. The counselors can also refer you to longer-term support options.

BLACK THERAPISTS / PSYCHOLOGISTS / ORGANIZATIONS FOCUSED ON THE MENTAL HEALTH OF BLACK BOYS

There is a stigma attached to mental health in the Black community. It can be difficult to seek out services when one risks the perception of being somehow broken or weak, especially for Black males. Mental illness is more prevalent in the Black community, in part, because Black people often avoid seeking out help when it is needed. Added to this stigma is the difficulty in locating a Black therapist or counselor who understands the unique challenges facing Black males. The following resources provide mental health support and, in some cases, free counseling with culturally relevant Black counselors.

- **Black Men Heal** provides access to mental health treatment, educational resources for Black therapists, and community resources for men of color. https://blackmenheal.org/.

- **Black Mental Wellness, Corp.** provides access to information on mental and behavioral health topics from a Black perspective to increase the diversity of mental health professionals and decrease the stigma surrounding mental health in the Black community. https://www.blackmentalwellness.com/.

- **Black Therapists Rock** (headquartered in Washington, DC) offers a directory of Black therapists and provides mental health awareness that addresses the impact of racial trauma. https://www.blacktherapistsrock.com/.

- **The Boris L. Henson Foundation**, founded by actress Taraji P. Henson in honor of her late father, Boris L. Henson, has a mission of breaking the stigma surrounding the seeking out of mental health services among Black people. They offer free online therapy. https://borislhensonfoundation.org.

- **Brother, You're on My Mind** is a fact sheet on depression and stress in younger Black males. https://www.nimhd.nih.gov/docs/byomm_factsheet05.pdf.

- **Institute of African American Mindfulness (IAAM)** is dedicated to building an inclusive community of mindful living within the Black community. https://www.iaam-dc.org/.

- **National Alliance on Mental Illness (NAMI)** offers information, crisis counseling, support, and education on mental illnesses. https://www.nami.org/.

- **Finding Mental Health Care that Fits Your Cultural Background** is a poster from NAMI that is specific to helping Black and Latinx families find therapists. https://www.nami.org/getmedia/96871c65-293b-42cb-9697-091897cfd8bd/flyer_culturallycompetentproviders2016.

- **The Steve Fund** offers an array of virtual and in-person programs and services designed to address the well-being of young Black people and ensure they have equal opportunities to thrive in academic and career pursuits. https://www.steve-fund.org/programs-services/.

- **Therapy for Black Men** offers referrals to Black counselors and seeks to break the stigma that asking for help is a sign of weakness. https://therapyforblackmen.org/.

APPS FOR BLACK MENTAL HEALTH

The modern digital age has made it easier to locate and utilize services with mobile apps. Below are mental health applications you may not have realized were available for download right to your phone.

- **Notes:** This app is already included with your phone. According to the University of Rochester Medical Center, journaling has many mental health benefits and can reduce anxiety and stress.[2] Using the notes app as a journal could help with this.

- **Headspace:** Headspace gives you tools to help you meditate and sleep more soundly. This is a paid app that costs $69.99 annually (with the first fourteen days free) or $12.99 a month (with the first 7 days free). Content wise, it is super user-friendly and there are sections for morning warm-up, sleep, general meditation, and focus. There are also games, and some of the exercises are led by Olympians Kim Glass and Leon Taylor.

- **Liberate: Black Meditation App:** While not quite as many users have reviewed this one, it is yet another option that centers Black mindfulness. LiberatePlus is the premium version of this app that costs either $71.99 yearly or $9.99 monthly. Liberate Plus offers a free seven-day trial. They will ask you how experienced you are with meditation, and you have access to three premium meditations before you start your free trial. All the meditations are five to twenty minutes long. You can favorite any of the meditations or activities to go back to in the future.

2   https://www.urmc.rochester.edu/encyclopedia/content.
    aspx?ContentID=4552&ContentTypeID=1

- **The Safe Place:** This a relatively unknown "Minority Mental Health app" that is averaging a rating of 4.6. In general, this app is more of a resource guide and has helpful information, including but not limited to racism during the pandemic, black mental health statistics, self-care tips, and inspirational black quotes. Additionally, the resources on this app are free and you do not need to register to use it, as it is free with or without an account.

- **Shine:** With membership to this app, you get "your own personalized self-care" for $64.99 annually (with the first seven days free). Without going premium, you have access to several free parts of the app, but paying for the app looks like it gets you *more* of everything (including music). The content they suggest for you is focused on your initial intention on signing up.

MENTAL HEALTH ADVOCATES FOR BLACK MALES

Mental health advocates are a vital resource for Black men and boys. They break the taboo of speaking about mental illness and let Black boys and men know it is okay to look for help when it's needed. Many of them set up organizations that help with referrals for health care or sponsor events. Either way, they are getting the word out about maintaining good mental hygiene and are a source of information for the community.

- **Anthony Duncan** is the co-founder of Dead the Silence, a social initiative he created in response to his sister's suicide in 2012, when he felt like he could not express his emotions. He advocates for Black men to speak about their emotions and discusses his own experience with depression. Duncan wants men to understand that it is okay to talk about their anxiety, depression, and other general emotions. http://www.deadthesilence.com/about/

- **Darian Hall** is a member of a Black fraternity and it inspired him to create change. He co-founded a company called Heal-Haus, which is focused on teaching meditation and maintaining the mental health of the Black community. It is based in New York, but they do live sessions online. https://www.healhaus.com/.

- **Jamie Hogue** grew up on the South Side of Chicago in housing projects, but he managed to work his way through graduate school, and became trained as a mental health practitioner. He works as an assistant principal in Carbondale, Illinois, and advocates for mental health services for Black males. He runs an organization called Mental Health Advocate for Black Males. Check out this article spotlighting Hogue in *Voyage LA*: http://voyagela.com/interview/meet-jamie-hogue-mental-health-advocate-black-males-im-based-chicago/

- **Brandon J. Johnson** is an advocate for Black mental health and for suicide prevention. Johnson has been featured in articles for Complex, *USA Today*, and *Johns Hopkins Magazine*. His videos on *The Black Mental Wellness Lounge* YouTube channel are informative. https://www.youtube.com/c/The-BlackMentalWellnessLounge/.

- **Lorenzo Lewis** is the founder of The Confess Project, which trains Black barbers to become mental health advocates and to offer their barbershops as safe spaces for Black males to discuss mental health issues. Lewis was born in prison, lost both of his parents at a young age, and was involved in gang activity as a teenager. He credits a barber with helping him seek out help for his adverse childhood experiences and turning his life around. He has given a TEDx Talk and has been featured widely in the media. https://www.theconfess-project.com/.

- **Jason Rosario** founded The Lives of Men, which seeks to create a new way of portraying Black masculinity to the world that disrupts the stereotypes we typically see in the media. Rosario is trying to help brands promote a more authentic voice for Black men. He founded his company in response to Black men being murdered by the police. http://www.the-livesofmen.com/.

- **Dr. Randy Sconiers**, who also goes by "Dr. S," is a mental health therapist who focuses on helping young Black men deal with the stereotypes that surround them and can cause them great mental anguish. He is also the host of *Mental-Hop with Dr. S*, a podcast that provides mental health education by utilizing hip-hop culture. *Mental-Hop* can be found on Apple Podcasts.

- **Dr. Erlanger Turner** is a licensed child psychologist and university professor based in Los Angeles. He writes a blog, *The Race to Good Health*, and has contributed as a mental health media expert for outlets such as *Oprah* magazine, *The Washington Post, Bustle*, and NBC News. Dr. Turner is also the host of *The Breakdown with Dr. Earl*, a mental health podcast. In 2020, he served as the President of the Society for Child and Family Policy and Practice and is the first Black male to be elected to this position. Dr. Turner has over ten years' experience treating children, adolescents, and adults with problems such as anxiety, depression, and stress. He specializes in the diagnosis and treatment of behavior disorders like Conduct Disorder, Oppositional Defiant Disorder, Attention-Deficit Hyperactivity Disorder (ADHD), and developmental disorders. He is the founder of the Instagram @TherapyforBlackKids.

- **Chance the Rapper:** In an article by *NBC News*, they discuss the highlights of Facebook Watch's "Peace of Mind With Taraji" interview with Chance, a musician and influencer. After one of his friends had a mental health crisis, he became an advocate for the mental health of Black men. Here is a link to that interview: https://fb.watch/9izeg9Mig_/

ORGANIZATIONS FOCUSED ON THE ACHIEVEMENT OF BLACK BOYS

Black boys are often overlooked when it comes to expectations for success. For example, they are less likely to take advanced placement courses in K–12 educational settings.[3] Organizations that encourage Black boys and their achievements are key to ensuring that they find success in their lives and grow as a result of mentorship. The following organizations encourage Black boys to strive harder.

- **AmeriCorps** is an organization of volunteers that works on many different projects throughout the United States, including in-school programs that support students in close to 12,000 schools. They also provide financial literacy training and help connect people to jobs. https://americorps.gov.

- **The Boys Initiative** is not limited to Black boys, but it seeks to close the gap between girls and boys, where boys underperform in every subject. They have resources and programs for parents and educators to help address the special needs of boys. https://boysinitiative.org/.

- **Career OneStop's Youth Program Finder** is an easily navigable site that provides information on youth programs close

---

3 https://edtrust.org/press-release/black-and-latino-students-shut-out-of-advanced-coursework-opportunities/

to you by searching a database of resources by zip code. They are focused on career exploration, training, and jobs. https://www.careeronestop.org/LocalHelp/EmploymentAndTraining/find-youth-programs.aspx

- **Concerned Black Men of America** provides mentoring, after school programs and scholarship opportunities for Black youth. They have chapters in many states. http://cbmnational.org/.

- **The City of Philadelphia Mayor's Office of Black Male Engagement** has a list of different educational resources for Black boys in Philadelphia. https://www.phila.gov/2018-06-11-education-resources-for-men-and-boys-of-color/.

- **Elevation Scholars** is a corporate philanthropy organization that helps high-achieving students from low-income families get into some of the best schools in the nation. Their focus is in Central Florida, but the potential for expansion into other areas is great. They also offer in-person workshops that help students write college essays, complete college applications, and write résumés. For inquiries, you can reach Lechon Cole at lcole@theelevationscgolars.org.

- **The Hidden Genius Project** trains and mentors Black boys in several different areas (including technology, entrepreneurship, and leadership skills) to help them transform their lives and communities. https://www.hiddengeniusproject.org.

- **The International Literacy Association (ILA)** works to ensure that children from all walks of life are literate. Their list of digital events may be useful to educators or those mentoring struggling readers. https://www.literacyworldwide.org/meetings-events/ila-digital-events.

- **JobCorps** is the largest nationwide residential career training program in the United States. They help youths aged sixteen to twenty-four obtain their high school diplomas, receive training for meaningful careers, and apply for employment assistance. https://www.jobcorps.gov.

- **National Youth Alliance for Boys & Men of Color** is an alliance of five different youth organizations committed to advancing the leadership of young Black men. https://fcyo.org/programs/national-youth-alliance-for-boys-and-men-of-color.

- **Philanthropy Massachusetts's Resources and Opportunities for Men & Boys of Color** is a list of scholarly articles and organizations dedicated to encouraging Black males to succeed. https://philanthropyma.org/resources-tools/resources-and-opportunity-boys-men-color.

BLACK INFLUENCERS FOCUSED ON BLACK ACHIEVEMENT

Nowadays, young people look to influencers as role models for encouragement. The next entry is an influencer who can have a positive effect on Black boys and young men.

- **Devale Ellis** is a former NFL player and actor who has become an internet sensation with his YouTube videos. With his wife Khadeen, he hosts a podcast called *Dead Ass*, which discusses love, sex, and marital issues. He has more than 369,000 subscribers on his YouTube channel, which addresses topics such as career success, balancing family life, and social media. He also regularly posts comedy skits on his YouTube vlog.

- **Tony A. Gaskins, Jr.,** is a celebrity life coach and intercontinental speaker. He started his first company, Soul Writer LLC, at the age of twenty-five and has built his brand from scratch. He is known for his love and relationship advice and is a highly sought after speaker who has addressed audiences on two continents and in over ten countries. He has authored close to twenty books on self-help and relationships.

- **Malcom "MJ" Harris** is an internationally recognized CEO, executive producer, and lifestyle business influencer. He has been featured in *Oprah, Market Watch, NB, USA Today,* and *Black Enterprise.* He has a global reach of more than 20 million people on social media and television. He began his career after growing up in a home surrounded by abuse and addiction, which serves as his lesson-building template for his viewers and listeners.

- **Rob Hill, Sr.,** also known as "the heart healer," is an author and entrepreneur. He has a social media following of nearly one million people. He is an international speaker on topics such as relationships, purpose-filled living, and community organizing. He is the author of several books, including *About Something Real, For Single People, I Got You,* and *Truce: Healing Your Heart After Disappointment.*

- **Stephan Labossiere** is a popular relationship coach on YouTube, with over 785k subscribers to his channel, *Stephan Speaks.* He is a great resource for teens who often struggle through adolescence with forming new and romantic relationships. Often, a cause for suicide in young men revolves around romantic relationships.

- **Trent Shelton** is a former NFL player who has become a ground-breaking motivational speaker and author. His YouTube videos have become viral sensations, and led him to an international career in motivational speaking. He hosts a podcast called *Straight Up with Trent Shelton* and has authored two books on reaching potential.

- **Eric Thomas, PhD**, is also known as "the Hip Hop Preacher." He is a critically acclaimed author, world-renowned speaker, educator, pastor, and was an audible.com Audie Award finalist. He teaches through a creative common-sense approach to living a successful and satisfying personal and professional life. Thomas has a large social media presence and tours regularly for public speaking events all around the world.

- **Michael Todd** is a bestselling author and the lead pastor at Transformation Church in Tulsa, Oklahoma. His passion is ministering to the lost and found for transformation. He is the author of three books, including *Crazy Faith*, *Relationship Goals*, and *Relationship Goals Challenge*. Todd speaks at a number of different events, conferences, and churches each year.

BLACK BOYS INTERESTED IN STEM

Black and Latinx workers are underrepresented in science, technology, engineering, and math fields. Black workers make up 11 percent of the overall workforce, but only 9 percent of STEM jobs, whereas white workers make up 63 percent of the STEM workforce. In some STEM-related fields such as engineering and architecture, this figure drops to just 5 percent of the workforce.[4] Black students are less likely to seek a degree in a STEM-related program as well. Black scientists have made amazing discoveries and inventions. It was a Black scientist who invented the bloodmobile (Dr. Charles Drew), a Black scientist who developed over 300 uses of peanuts and pioneered methods to avoid soil depletion (George Washington Carver), and a Black scientist who first synthesized cortisone, steroids, and birth control pills from plants (Dr. Percy Julian). The

---

4   https://www.pewresearch.org/social-trends/2018/01/09/diversity-in-the-stem-workforce-varies-widely-across-jobshttps://www.pewresearch.org/social-trends/2018/01/09/diversity-in-the-stem-workforce-varies-widely-across-jobs/

following resources help encourage Black boys and young men to pursue an interest in STEM studies.

- **Black Boys Code** looks to improve the future of Black youth through education in computer science and technology. They have eleven chapters in Canada and one in the United States, with plans to expand soon. This is a great program for boys interested in computer gaming and coding. https://www.blackboyscode.com/.

- **Black Enterprise** has a list of the top five STEM job options for Black men (of course, women could also pursue these careers). https://www.blackenterprise.com/jobs-stem-science-tech-black-male-employment/.

- **National Society of Black Engineers** holds a summer camp in several different US cities each year. About 300 kids can attend this free program. The society seeks to increase the number of Black engineering students in America. https://seek.nsbe.org/.

- **SciStarter** has a website with a searchable database of science projects happening online or near you. https://scistarter.org/finder.

SCHOLARSHIPS

According to UNCF, even before they get to college, Black male students are at a disadvantage compared to students of other races. Only 57 percent of Black students have access to the college prep courses they'll need to succeed in college, compared to 81 percent of Asian students and 71 percent of white students. Black students who take the ACT exam perform more poorly on the test as well, with 61 percent of them failing to meet any of the four ACT benchmarks compared to 31 percent of all other students. Once in college, Black students are also more likely to have to enroll in remedial courses.[5]

There are barriers to the success of Black male students in college as well. Without good test scores, the rest of the application process becomes more difficult, and they are less likely to earn scholarships. Black men have the lowest completion rate of anyone: only 40 percent of them earn a college degree in six years. The high dropout rate for Black males can be attributed to the fact that many are older, independent students (65 percent), who must balance work and family life with a college course load.[6]

Black students are also more likely to attend for-profit institutions rather than public universities, which sets them up for a large load of debt. Studies have shown that scholarship opportunities that help lighten the burden of student debt are key factors in the success of Black students. The following is a list of funding opportunities for college, often paired with mentorship and other programs that increase the likelihood of academic success.

- **Beyoncé's About Love Scholarship** program awards $2 million to students enrolled in arts and creative programs at HBCUs. https://www.beyonce.com/image/the-about-love-scholarship/.

- **Best Colleges** has a comprehensive list of scholarships for Black students, many of them in the STEM fields. https://www.bestcolleges.com/financial-aid/african-american-scholarships/.

- **The Frederick Douglass Bicentennial Scholarship Program** awards $20,000 in scholarships to students enrolled at Histor-

---

5   https://uncf.org/pages/k-12-disparity-facts-and-stats
6   https://uncf.org/the-latest/african-americans-and-college-education-by-the-numbers

ically Black Colleges and Universities. https://uncf.org/pages/the-frederick-douglass-bicentennial-scholarship-program

- **The Jackie Robinson Foundation** provides financial assistance and helps guide Black students through the process of higher education. https://jackierobinson.org/apply/.

- **The National Black Child Development Institute (NBCDI)** provides scholarships for Black students enrolled in Early Childhood Education. https://www.nbcdi.org/what-we-do/early-childhood-education.

- **The United Negro College Fund (UNCF)** is the largest minority education organization. They provide scholarships and other programs to students at thirty-seven member colleges and universities. www.uncf.org.

- **The UNCF/Koch Scholars Program** offers scholarships, mentorship, academic and professional support, and networking opportunities to talented undergraduate Black students. There is a focus on entrepreneurship among the scholarship recipients. https://uncf.org/programs/uncf-koch-scholars-program.

- **Other Listings for Scholarships for Black students:**

  - https://bold.org/scholarships/scholarships-for-black-students/

  - https://www.usnews.com/education/best-colleges/paying-for-college/articles/where-to-find-scholarships-for-black-students

  - https://www.goingmerry.com/blog/african-american-scholarships/

  - https://uncf.org/pages/the-frederick-douglass-bicentennial-scholarship-program

HISTORICALLY BLACK COLLEGES AND UNIVERSITIES AND BLACK FRATERNITIES

Attending a Historically Black College or University (HBCU) can be a transformative experience for a young Black man, and it is often one of the few places they can find themselves in the majority when it comes to race. Born out of necessity because of segregation after the Civil War, HBCUs have nurtured some of the country's greatest minds and given thousands of Black students alma maters that understand their cultural and social needs, as well as academic freedom. According to UNCF, Black students at HBCUs thrive more easily and tend to be more successful at graduating than they do at non-HBCUs. UNCF scholarship recipients have a 70 percent six-year graduation rate, compared to 45.9 percent who do not attend HBCUs. On average, the cost of attending an HBCU is 28 percent less than attending other colleges, and 40 percent of HBCU students report feeling financially secure compared to 29 percent of Black students at other colleges. Although HBCUs make up just 3 percent of the nation's colleges and universities, they enroll 10 percent of all Black college students and account for 20 percent of all Black graduates. An HBCU graduate can expect to earn an additional $927,000 in their lifetime, 56 percent more than they would earn with a degree from a non-HBCU.[7]

Black fraternities also offer support to young Black male students. In addition to the social support, they offer networking opportunities with successful alumni, as well as experience in community building and volunteerism. Inter-collegiate fraternal alliances ensure that there is a global network of brethren looking to support each other. Some Black fraternities include:

---

7   https://uncf.org/the-latest/why-hbcus-still-matter

- **Alpha Phi Alpha** is the first intercollegiate Greek-lettered Black fraternity. They were founded in 1906 at Cornell University.

- **Iota Phi Theta** was founded at Morgan State University in 1963. It is the fifth largest Greek-lettered Black fraternity.

- **Kappa Alpha Psi** is the oldest Black Greek-lettered fraternity west of the Appalachian Mountains, founded in 1911 at Indiana University Bloomington.

- **Omega Psi Phi** was founded in 1911 at Howard University. It is the first fraternal organization founded at an HBCU.

- **Phi Beta Sigma** was founded in 1914 at Howard University. The fraternity seeks to embody the ideals of brotherhood, scholarship, and service. They are dedicated to serving the community as opposed to having an exclusive purpose.

Here is some information about a few of the HBCUs and the fraternities operating on their campuses.

- **Delaware State University:** Founded in 1891, Delaware State University has a beautiful 356-acre pedestrian campus with more than fifty buildings and four athletic facilities. The school maintains a fleet of airplanes for its Airway Science Programs. Fraternities active at Delaware State include:

  - Alpha Phi Alpha
  - Omega Psi Phi
  - Phi Beta Sigma
  - Iota Phi Theta
  - https://www.desu.edu

- **Fisk University:** Fisk University was founded in Nashville in 1865, within six months of the end of the Civil War, and just a couple of years after the Emancipation Proclamation was signed. They have a partnership with Vanderbilt University. Fraternities active at Fisk include:

    - Alpha Phi Alpha
    - Kappa Alpha Psi
    - Omega Psi Phi
    - Phi Beta Sigma
    - https://www.fisk.edu

- **Florida A&M University:** Founded in 1887, with two instructors and fifteen students, Florida A&M University was named the #1 HBCU by 2022 *U.S. News and World Report*.[8] Fraternities active at Florida A&M include:

    - Alpha Phi Alpha
    - Iota Phi Theta
    - Phi Beta Sigma
    - Omega Psi Phi
    - http://www.famu.edu

- **Howard University:** Founded in Washington, DC, in 1867, Howard University has awarded more than 120,000 degrees in the arts, the sciences, and the humanities. Fraternities active at Howard include:

    - Alpha Phi Alpha
    - Iota Phi Theta

---

8   https://www.blackenterprise.com/famu-ranked-no-1-public-hbcu-for-third-year-in-a-row-new-guidebook-reveals/

- Kappa Alpha Psi

- Omega Psi Phi

- Phi Beta Sigma

- https://howard.edu

ACTIVE/PROMINENT BLACK STUDENT UNIONS

Black student unions help advocate for Black student bodies at institutions of higher learning. They also offer a place for Black students to socialize and discuss matters of importance to them. Black student unions have been instrumental in shaping college policies and changing those that do not serve Black students. The following are organizations that cater to the needs of Black students.

- **National Black Student Alliance:** Founded by Skye Jackson, this organization helps Black students find allies within their schools and communities, offering a sense of camaraderie. Jackson made news for being one of three students to start the "Black at" hashtag on Instagram, where Black students relate their experiences being Black at different schools. https://www.nationalbsa.org/.

- **National Black Student Union (NBSU):** This organization holds an annual conference of Black student leaders from across the nation. They also have other events, some of them held online. https://www.facebook.com/nbsuconference/.

MEDIA

For many years, the media was controlled by white interests and depicted Black men and boys in a stereotypical fashion. Whether it was Stepin Fetchit or a hyper-masculinized Black archetype, Black masculinity has taken a beating in the media. The importance of realistic role models for young Black boys cannot be overestimated. The following resources depict Black people in nuanced, complex ways that showcase our strengths, and then complicate them by clearly admitting our weaknesses.

Documentaries, Films, and TV Shows

- *13th*, a documentary directed by Ava Duverney, explores the industrial prison complex and how it profits off the incarceration of Black boys and young men. It is available to stream on Netflix.

- *Black Boys* is a streaming show that explores Black masculinity in America and the racial legacy that has impacted it. It is available to stream on Peacock.

- On *Bookmarks*, celebrity readers share children's books by Black authors to spark conversations about empathy, equality, self-love, and antiracism.

- *Colin in Black & White*, narrated by Colin Kaepernick, is a dramatic series that relates his experiences with class, culture, and color growing up while aspiring for greatness. It is available to stream on Netflix.

- *Eyes on the Prize* is an award-winning PBS documentary chronicling the history of civil rights.

- *Good Hair* is a humorous film in which Chris Rock explores the Black hair industry and why our hair is considered "not good" by beauty standards.

- *Hair Love,* directed by Matthew A. Cherry, is an Oscar-winning short film about a little girl and her father and their attempts to style her hair.

- *I Am Not Your Negro* is a documentary on James Baldwin, as he explores the history of race in America and reflects the current systemic racism with his unfinished novel, *Remember This House*. It is narrated by Samuel L. Jackson.

- *The Wonder Years* (2021) is a reimagining of the popular 1990s sitcom. In this updated version, a Black man recalls his experiences growing up in late 1960s Montgomery, Alabama. It is available to stream on Hulu.

- The Voice of Black Cincinnati provides **a list of the best Netflix movies for Black kids**. https://thevoiceofblackcincinnati.com/black-movies-for-kids-on-netflix/

Podcasts

- *Black Zen* is a podcast that aims to break down the financial barrier that prevents many Black people from practicing mindful meditation in a non-religious approach. https://www.blackzen.co/#bz-podcast.

- *Our Mental Health Minute: Session Notes*, hosted by Ri and CT, are short discussions on matters of Black mental health with leading experts. https://podcasts.apple.com/us/podcast/our-mental-health-minute-session-notes/id1493833007.

Books, Audiobooks, and Essays

You cannot rely on your child's school library to provide them with books and audiobooks that reflect their cultural heritage and an accurate history. With the movement to ban Critical Race Theory gaining momentum around the country, it is important to provide Black boys (who tend to score lower on reading exams)[9] with reading material that gives them a better understanding of the past and present, as well as a vision for the future.

Elementary

- *All Because You Matter,* by **Tami Charles.** This picture book is a lyrical love letter that explains that Black children matter.

- *All the Colors We Are: The Story of How We Get Our Skin Color,* by **Katie Kissinger.** This children's picture book (for ages three and up) examines skin color with an eye for understanding differences.

- *Child of the Civil Rights Movement,* by **Paula Young Shelton.** A book for children ages four to eight, this is an intimate look at the birth of the civil rights movement.

- *The Courageous Adventures of the Konscious Kidz,* by **John Casselberry and Madeline Connor.** Konscious Kidz (for ages six to eleven) is a five-book series with twenty-four stories about a culturally diverse group of six neighborhood kids.

- *Crown: An Ode to the Fresh Cut* by **Derrick Barnes** is a celebration of the barbershop and the confidence a fresh haircut bestows on Black boys.

9 https://www.kqed.org/news/11501627/data-exclusive-75-percent-of-black-california-boys-dont-meet-state-reading-standards

- *Daddy, There's a Noise Outside,* **by Kenneth Braswell.** This children's picture book (for ages six to eleven) tells the story of what happens when a noise outside wakes two children in their inner-city home.

- *Hey You!: An Empowering Celebration of Growing Up Black,* **by Dapo Adeola.** This children's picture book (for ages four to eight) is a lyrical, inspirational exploration of growing up Black.

- *I Am Every Good Thing* **by Derrick Barnes** is a lyrical exploration of what makes one Black boy great.

- *I Am Jackie Robinson,* **by Brad Meltzer.** Pro-baseball legend Jackie Robinson in the subject of this picture biography for kids (ages four to seven).

- In *The King of Kindergarten* **by Derrick Barnes**, a confident little boy takes pride in his first day of kindergarten.

- In *Just for You! The Low-Down, Bad-Day Blues* **by Derrick Barnes**, a boy having a difficult day discovers what a difference his attitude can make.

- *Let's Talk About Race,* **by Julius Lester.** This children's picture book (for ages four to seven) encourages kids to talk about differences. It is an excellent springboard for discussions on race.

- *The Other Side,* **by Jacqueline Woodson.** Two children, one Black, one white, strike up a friendship in a segregated town in this children's picture book (for ages five to eight).

- *Rosa,* **by Nikki Giovanni.** This book (for ages eight to ten) tells the story of Rosa Parks and her refusal to give up her seat on a segregated bus.

- *Separate Is Never Equal: Sylvia Mendez and Her Family's Fight for Desegregation,* **by Duncan Tonatiuh.** This children's book (for ages six to nine) tells the story of Sylvia

Mendez, who was denied a spot in a whites only school in California, and her legal battle to end segregation in schools in the state.

- *Something Happened in our Town: A Child's Story About Racial Injustice,* by **Marianne Celano, PhD.** This children's novel (for ages four to eight) follows two families—one Black, one white—in the aftermath of the shooting of a Black man. It seeks to answer questions about racial injustice that young kids may have.

- *The Stone Thrower,* by **Jael Ealey Richardson.** This picture book (for ages four to nine) tells the story of football player Chuck Ealey, who grew up in a segregated neighborhood of Portsmouth, Ohio. Despite being a phenomenal football player, Chuck Ealey never played pro-football.

- *The Story of Ruby Bridges,* by **Robert Coles.** The story of the little girl who desegregated a school in the South (for ages three and up).

- *Viola Desmond Won't Be Budged!,* by **Jody Nyasha Warner.** This picture book (for ages eight to nine) tells the story of Viola Desmond, a Black Canadian woman who refused to give up her movie theater seat in the 1940s.

- *What's the Difference? Being Different is Amazing,* by **Doyin Richards.** This children's book (for ages two to ten) celebrates diversity.

Middle School

- *Becoming Muhammad Ali* by **James Patterson and Kwame Alexander** explores the childhood of Cassius Clay.

- *Black Boy Joy: 17 Stories Celebrating Black Boyhood,* **edited by Kwame Mbalia.** Seventeen notable Black authors celebrate Black boyhood in this anthology of fiction.

- *Class Act,* **by Jerry Craft.** This graphic novel explores friendship and the experience of being one of the few kids of color at a prestigious private school.

- *Darius & Twig* **by Walter Dean Myers** is a 2014 Coretta Scott King Honor Book. It tells the story of a pair of friends who are exploring the meaning of friendship and living one's own path.

- *Dear Martin,* **by Nic Stone.** This novel tackles racism and centers on a young Black boy who begins a journal writing to Dr. Martin Luther King, Jr.

- *The Freedom Writers Diary,* **by The Freedom Writers with Erin Gruwell.** The twentieth anniversary edition of the classic book tells the story of a dedicated teacher and the remarkable group of students she inspired.

- *New Kid,* **by Jerry Craft.** This graphic novel follows seventh grader Jordan Banks on his journey as the new kid at a prestigious private school. Jordan is one of the few kids of color in his entire grade.

- *Stamped: Racism, Antiracism, and You,* **by Jason Reynolds and Ibram X. Kendi.** This reimagining of Ibram X. Kendi's National Book Award-winning *Stamped: From the Beginning* explores the legacy of racism and looks to the future.

- *Swing* **by Kwame Alexander and Mary Rand Hess** is a novel in verse that explores love, relationships, and why Black Lives Matter.

- *The Watsons Go to Birmingham—1963,* **by Christopher Paul Curtis.** This classic children's novel is about an unforgettable family on a road trip to Birmingham, Alabama in 1963.

Young Adults

- *All American Boys,* **by Jason Reynolds and Brendan Kiely.** This novel for teens explores the repercussions of a single violent act on two boys (one Black, one white), their community, and ultimately, the nation.

- *Battle Cry: Waging and Winning the War Within,* **by Jason Wilson.** Wilson calls on readers to redefine masculinity and master their emotions.

- *Black and Resilient: 52 Weeks of Anti-Racist Activities for Black Joy and Empowerment,* **by M.J. Fievre.** This guidebook has anti-racist activities, affirmation, and lessons every Black boy needs.

- *Cry like a Man: Fighting for Freedom from Emotional Incarceration,* **by Jason Wilson.** A leader in teaching transformation to boys and young men in Detroit, Wilson tells his own story of discovering what it means to "be a man."

- *Ghost Boys,* **by Jewell Parker Rhodes.** This heart-breaking story of a Black boy killed by police officers draws connections to other murdered boys throughout history.

- *The Hate U Give,* **by Angie Thomas.** Protests erupt when a young girl witnesses the police shooting of one of her friends in this young adult novel.

- *Letters to a Young Brother: Manifest Your Destiny,* **by Hill Harper.** This book of inspirational letters offers advice to boys and young men in a down-to-earth style.

- *Long Way Down,* **by Jason Reynolds.** This is the #1 *New York Times* bestselling, award-winning novel reimagined as a graphic novel.

- *March,* **by John Lewis and Andrew Aydin.** *March* is a first-hand account of John Lewis's struggle for civil and human rights. It is a trilogy of graphic novels.

- *On the Come Up,* **by Angie Thomas.** An ode to hip hop, this book tells the story of a girl with the odds stacked against her.

- *This Book is Anti-Racist,* **by Tiffany Jewell.** In this book for the young person who doesn't know how to speak up against racial injustice, Jewell writes about racism and how to undo it.

- *Walk Boldly,* **by M.J. Fievre.** In this guidebook for teens, Black boys can explore the factors keeping them from living an authentic life.

Books for Parents and Mentors

- *Between the World and Me,* **by Ta-Nehisi Coates.** A bold and necessary literary exploration of Black history, this book is also a winner of the National Book Award.

- *Black Stats: African Americans by the Numbers in the Twenty-first Century,* **by Monique W. Morris.** This is an exploration of the problem of systemic racism, as explained by the statistics surrounding the issue.

- *How to Be an Antiracist,* **by Ibram X. Kendi.** This guidebook explains racism and how to oppose it.

- *The Invention of the White Race,* **by Theodore W. Allen.** This book's thesis is that the white race was socially constructed to create class conflict.

- *The New Jim Crow: Mass Incarceration in the Age of Color-blindness,* **by Michelle Alexander.** This book examines mass incarceration and the consequences for the Black community.

- *Parenting for Liberation: A Guide for Raising Black Children,* **by Trina Greene Brown.** This guidebook offers helpful exercises for raising Black children through the lens of liberation rather than fear.

- *Raising Black Boys,* by Dr. Jawanza Kunjufu. Filled with useful tips, this book helps parents avoid the pitfalls of raising Black sons.

- *So You Want to Talk About Race,* by Ijeoma Oluo. This book is a revelatory examination of race in America.

- *Tears We Cannot Stop: A Sermon to White America,* by Michael Eric Dyson. This, too, is a frank and searing discussion on race in America.

- *Uncomfortable Conversations with a Black Man* by Emmanuel Acho is an excellent resource guide to learning how to have conversations about race.

- *White Fragility: Why It's So Hard for White People to Talk About Racism,* by Robin DiAngelo. This in-depth discussion of the causes of white fragility explores how to get around it to build a better future.

- *White Rage: The Unspoken Truth of Our Racial Divide,* by Carol Anderson, PhD. This book looks at the history of racism in America and examines the forces that keep it in power.

- *Your Black Friend and Other Strangers,* by Ben Passmore. This is a collection of culturally charged comics.

Book Lists

- **The Brown Bookshelf** has a collection of books that include brown and Black protagonists who deal at times with tough issues. www.thebrownbookshelf.com.

- **Common Sense Media** (a nonprofit that rates movies, TV shows, books, apps and other media for parents and schools) has curated a list of eighty books with diverse, multicultural characters for kids of all ages. www.commonsensemedia.org/lists/books-with-characters-of-color.

- *The New York Times* curated their own list: "These Books Can Help You Explain Racism and Protest to Your Kids." www.nytimes.com/2020/06/03/parenting/kids-books-racism.html.

- *Good Housekeeping* and **PBS Kids** also have lists of kids' books that can help start the conversation about race.

  - "16 Children's Books to Help Support Conversations on Race and Racial Injustice": https://www.goodhousekeeping.com/uk/lifestyle/editors-choice-book-reviews/g32754174/childrens-books-about-race/

  - "18 Children's Books to Prompt and Further Conversations on Race": https://www.pbs.org/education/blog/18-childrens-books-to-prompt-and-further-conversations-on-race

- **Social Justice Books** offers a valuable selection of multicultural and social justice books (including Afro-Latinx titles) for children, YA, and educators. www.socialjusticebooks.org.

Other Videos, Songs, and Read-Aloud Books

- *Back of the Bus*, **by Aaron Reynolds.** This tells the story of the Rosa Parks bus incident from the point of view of a boy who is also on the bus.

- *Bippity Bop Barbershop*, **by Natasha Anastasia Tarpley.** This is a familiar story about a rite of passage, as Miles's father takes him to the barbershop for the first time.

- *The Case for Loving—The Fight for Interracial Marriage*, **by Selina Alko.** A children's book about the Loving family, who won a Supreme Court case for interracial marriage in the miscegenated South.

- **"The Color of Me."** This *Sesame Street* song explores differences in skin color.

- *Don't Touch My Hair!*, **by Sharee Miller.** In this story, a young girl learns to set boundaries with those who want to touch her hair.

- *Feast for 10*, **by Cathryn Falwell.** This rhyming children's book is about a Black family who prepare a meal for ten.

- *Henry's Freedom Box*, **by Ellen Levine.** This is the stirring true story about a slave who mails himself to freedom.

- *I Am Enough*, **by Grace Byers.** Written by a multi-racial child of deaf parents, this book seeks to solve the problem of bullying.

- **"I Love My Hair" (bilingual).** This Sesame Street song is a musical celebration of Black hair.

- **"Jump Shamador" (activist song).** This is a Jamaican children's song.

- *Let the Children March*, **by Monica Clark-Robinson.** Told through the story of the Children's Crusade, this story aims to tell children that they are beautiful and that their voices have power.

- *Moses: When Harriet Tubman Led Her People to Freedom*, **by Carole Boston Weatherford.** This is a tribute to Harriet Tubman, who was nicknamed "Moses" for her work on the Underground Railroad.

- **"What I Am."** Will.i.am. joins the *Sesame Street* Muppets for this inspirational song about individuality.

Essays

- **"Mindful While Black," by Paul Singleton III.** In this essay for the On Being Project, Singleton reflects on his life as a Black man.

- **"Scenes From a Life in Negroland," by Margo Jefferson.** Jefferson reflects on life as an upper middle class Black girl in this essay for *Guernica Magazine*.

- **"This Is the Black Renaissance," by Ibram X. Kendi.** This piece for *TIME Magazine* examines the new Black Renaissance that encompasses art, culture, politics, and more.

- **"The Word Is 'Nemesis': The Fight to Integrate the National Spelling Bee, by Cynthia R. Greenlee.** In this longform piece for *Bunk*, Greenlee looks at the surprising history of the National Spelling Bee.

OTHER RESOURCES

Toys

- **Blacktoystore.com** is an excellent resource for finding Black-owned toy companies and toys made for Black children. From dolls and action figures to STEM-related play, they have it all.

- **Pattycake Doll Company** specializes in bringing diversity to your toybox.

- **People Colors Crayons** come in a variety of skin colors.

- **Sugarfoot Rag Dolls** come in all races and ethnicities.

Webinars and Classes

Webinars and online classes are a great way to educate yourself further and gain specific parenting insights relevant to your Black child. You can attend from the comfort of your own home, and you don't even have to change out of your house clothes to do so.

- **Colin Kaepernick's Know Your Rights Camp** for Black children teaches them how to know their rights, exercise them, and interact with law enforcement in different scenarios.

- **EmbraceRace's "Moving 'The Talk' to 'The Walk' for Black Children" Webinar**, with Drs. Riana Elyse Anderson and Shawn C. T. Jones, details how to move on from talking about race with practical tips on how to handle racist situations. EmbraceRace has several webinars that may be of interest to you. It is hosted by a couple who are Black parents themselves, and each webinar features leading experts in their field.

Resources for Parents of Black Children

As a parent, you'll want all the tools you can find. These next resources are for parents of Black children and their families. Several of the following resources are paid programs, but even the paid programs have useful information on their websites, often free.

- **CICC's Effective Black Parenting Program (EBPP)** utilizes the work of Black scholars to help you become a better parent. There are a couple of course offerings, which require homework. Visit https://www.effectiveblackparenting.com/.

- *Do Right by Me: Learning to Raise Black Children in White Spaces,* **by Kathryn D'Angelo and Valerie Harrison**, explores parenting a biracial child when you are white.

- **Dr. Ann-Louise Lockhart's "Parenting Teens, Tweens and Everything in Between" course** is geared toward parents of tweens and teens. Dr. Lockhart is a Black pediatric psychologist. https://parenting-teens-tweens-and-everything-in-betwe.teachable.com.

- *Raising Confident Black Kids,* **by M.J. Fievre**, is a comprehensive guidebook is for teachers and parents of Black children. It is an invaluable resource in raising and mentoring confident Black kids.

- **Raising Equity** is a website that provides free videos and resources to parents on how to fight racism and cultivate an open mind in themselves and their kids. Visit https://raisingequity.org/.

- **Strong African American Families (SAAF)**, put together by the Center for Family Research at the University of Georgia, is a for-pay program that will help you build a stronger family. Visit https://cfr.uga.edu/saaf-programs/saaf/.

Resources for Educating Black Children

Homeschooling is becoming a popular option for many parents of Black children. Between the poor performance of public school systems in educating Black children and the recent pandemic, many parents have found they have all they need right at home to provide their children an enriching, safe, culturally relevant homeschool experience. These resources provide you with materials to use in your homeschool classroom, or to expand your understanding of the educational process. If you are a teacher in a school setting, you may find some useful information here as well.

- **Black Boys in Crisis Resources & Activities Center** is a list of valuable resources for homeschoolers. They are dedicated to improving the plight of young Black boys. https://black-boysincrisis.com/resources-activities/.

- **"Black Boys Matter: Cultivating Their Identity, Agency, and Voice"** is an article from The National Association for the Education of Young Children (NAEYC) that discusses how to get Black children motivated in the classroom and how to keep them motivated. Read the article at https://www.naeyc.org/resources/pubs/tyc/feb2019/black-boys-matter.

- **"Black Boys Matter: Strategies for a Culturally Responsive Classroom"** is a second article from NAEYC that offers strategies for building a culturally responsive classroom. Read the article at https://www.naeyc.org/resources/pubs/tyc/apr2019/strategies-culturally-responsive-classroom.

- **Black Men Read** offers Black male mentors to Black children, as well as opportunities to be read to. www.bmrkids.org.

- **Kahoot!** curated a list of different kids activities for Black History Month. https://kahoot.com/blog/2018/02/05/black-history-month-activities-kahoot/

- **Tinybeans** has a list of twenty-eight Black History Month resources for kids of all ages. https://tinybeans.com/black-history-month/.

- *Spare the Kids: Why Whupping Children Won't Save Black America,* **by Stacey Patton**, is a challenge to the notion of corporal punishment that is so common in Black homes.

Afrocentric Homeschooling Resources

- *Brown Mamas' 20-Day Guide to DeSchooling Workbook,* **by Muffy Malousa**, shows you how to make homeschooling easy for you and your children.

- **A2Z Homeschooling** has many resources for homeschooling parents including this guide to Afrocentric homeschooling. https://a2zhomeschooling.com/religion/afrocentric-home-schooling-black-children/.

- **Education for Life Academy** offers many resources including this African history guide. The site is for homeschooling parents and teachers. https://educationforlifeacademy.com/.

- *The Homeschool Alternative: Incorporating a Homeschool Mindset for the Benefit of Black Children in America* ,by **Dr. Myiesha Taylor and Haley Taylor Schlitz**, is part how-to guide for Black homeschooling parents/part memoir fusion about the homeschooling journey for one Black family.

- **The Historic Journey** provides a detailed curriculum about Black history through the focal point of President Barack Obama's election. https://thehistoricjourney.org/.

- **The Intuitive Homeschooler** has a comprehensive list of homeschooling resources, including Afrocentric homeschooling guides. https://theintuitivehomeschooler.com/2018/11/30/aafrican-centered-homeschool-curriculum/.

- **Black Homeschool Families** and **Homeschooling for Black Freethinkers** Facebook groups.

- **"Master World Class Schooling,"** a mini course offered by Sakilé, a homeschooling parent who travels the world while teaching her six children. www.embraceyourfree.com.

- *The Mom Trotter's* **Comprehensive Resource Guide For Black Homeschooling Families** offers resources to help raise educated global citizens.

After-School Programs that Promote Achievement

After-school programs can be instrumental in raising a healthy, happy Black child. Many Black children have no parent at home when they arrive from school, and left to their own devices, the experience of a latchkey kid can be isolating and fraught with boredom. Many of these programs offer tutoring, sports activities, and other educational resources as well as fun!

- **The After School Alliance** offers hands-on programs that teach children about STEM. https://afterschoolalliance.org/AA3PM/#resources.

- **American Youth Football** has flag football leagues for kids of all ages. The program charges money for their services, but scholarships are available to some applicants. https://www.americanyouthfootball.com/football/.

- **Big Brothers Big Sisters of America** pairs your child with an adult mentor. https://www.bbbs.org/.

- **The Boys & Girls Club of America** has club locations in all fifty states, Puerto Rico, the Virgin Islands, and US Military Bases. Each club has different programs to meet the needs of their children locally, but they have national programs for sports and recreation, as well as health and nutrition. https://www.bgclubs.org/.

- **"More Black Men Embracing Yoga to Ease Emotional Stress"** is an article about Black yoga instructors and how they are broadening their services to attract male clients. Read the article at https://www.nbcnews.com/news/nbcblk/more-black-men-embracing-yoga-ease-emotional-stress-n1100836.

LGBTQIA+ Resources for Families

If you are the parent of an LGBTQIA+ child, you probably already know the taboo surrounding Blacks who identify as queer. This taboo leaves queer Black youth particularly vulnerable to homophobic violence and feelings of despair. Coming out can be particularly difficult for Black adolescents. These resources will help you adjust to the coming out process and support your child as they mature.

- **"Coming Out: Information for Parents of LGBTQ Teens"** is a guide by The American Academy of Pediatrics to the coming out process and what you can do to help support your child as they forge their identity. https://www.healthychildren.org/English/ages-stages/teen/dating-sex/Pages/Four-Stages-of-Coming-Out.aspx.

- **Family Equality** is all about achieving equality for LGBTQIA+ families and meeting people who are in similar family situations. https://www.familyequality.org/.

- **Reclaim** partners with queer youth aged thirteen to twenty-five and helps them reclaim their lives from oppression. They help increase access to mental health services. https://www.reclaim.care/.

- **The National Queer and Trans Therapists of Color Network** refers therapists for people of color in the LGBTQIA+ community. https://nqttcn.com/en/.

- **The Maven Leadership Collective** consistently invests in creative social impact leaders who are queer, trans people of color, and their allies to build communities that thrive even in the face of crisis, transition, and tragedy. https://mavenleadership.org/about-us/.

Black Churches and Community Centers

Black churches and church youth groups are an integral part of the Black community and can help provide your child with a morally based community of support. Many offer youth programs and are sources of not only inspiration, but also of history on the struggle of Black Americans. If you are not already a member of a Black church, check your local congregation.

- **The 16th Street Baptist Church** is a historic church in Birmingham, Alabama, that was the site of the KKK bombing in 1963 that killed four young girls and injured more than twenty congregants. The church, which was a key meeting ground during the Civil Rights Movement, is still open and holds many different events.

- **"Not by Bread Alone: The Role of the African American Church in Inner-City Development"** is a Brookings Institute report about Black churches. Read the report at https://www.brookings.edu/articles/not-by-bread-alone-the-role-of-the-african-american-church-in-inner-city-development/.

- **"Why The Black Church Is Vital For Healthy Communities"** is an article on *Shared Justice* about the important role Black churches play in the community. It is available at https://www.sharedjustice.org/domestic-justice/2017/12/20/why-the-black-church-is-vital-for-healthy-communities.

Magazine and Box Subscriptions

A fun way to help educate your child is through subscription boxes. The following are some subscriptions you may find useful.

- **Blacklisted** is focused on promoting cultures that are black-listed from the classroom. Their subscription boxes contain books by Black authors.

- **Call Number** is a quarterly library-inspired book subscription box that curates a reading list of newly released Black authors for you.

- *Ebony*, the titular magazine of Black culture, tells the stories of Black America for Black America.

- **Just Like Me Box** service curates books for your child based on their age. As your child ages, the books become more advanced.

- *Ourselves Black* is an online and print magazine devoted to issues of Black mental health.

Programs You Might Be Interested In

- **Health and Resilience Project (HARP)**, run through the University of Georgia, offers Black families $850 to take part in their research into Black health and resilience.

- **Mindfulness Resource for People of Color** is a comprehensive list of articles and resources for the Black community. https://www.detroitk12.org/cms/lib/MI50000060/Centricity/Domain/41/Mindfulness%20Resource%20for%20People%20of%20Color.pdf.

Home and Neighborhood Safety Resources for Children

If your child plays outside in your neighborhood, keeping them and the neighborhood safe is an added concern. They'll need to know how to fend for themselves when you're not with them. The following online guides can help you learn to keep your family safe:

- **"At Home Alone: A Parent's Guide."** If your children are at the age where they can be left alone, you'll want to reference this National Crime Prevention Council (NCPC) guide for resources to help them stay safe. http://archive.ncpc.org/resources/files/pdf/neighborhood-safety/chalone.pdf.

- **"Kidzworld Neighborhood Safety Tips."** Designed for children, this guide helps them learn tips on how to be safe in their neighborhood and when home alone. www.kidzworld.com/article/8122-neighborhood-safety-tips.

- **"Neighborhood Safety Tips for Parents."** This step-by-step guide by the NCPC can help you keep your kids and neighborhood safe. https://www.ncpc.org/resources/home-neighborhood-safety/neighborhood-safety-tips-for-parents/.

- **"The Smart Route to Bicycle Safety."** This guide is also put out by the NCPC and helps teach your child bicycle safety, as well as how to avoid having their bicycle stolen. http://archive.ncpc.org/resources/files/pdf/neighborhood-safety/bikesafety04.pdf.

- **"Ten New Neighborhood Safety Tips."** From the National Center for Missing and Exploited Children, this guide is for those moving to a new neighborhood. The tips here will help you make simple rules to ensure a safe new home. www.parents.com/kids/safety/tips/10-new-neighborhood-safety-tips/.

Other Resources:

Here are some other resources that can come in handy whether you're just starting to think about the safety of your neighborhood or you've been a long-time community organizer:

- **"Eight Simple Ways to Your Neighborhood Safer."** These tips from SafeWise explain how you and your neighbors can work together to fight criminal activity in your community. https://www.safewise.com/blog/8-simple-ways-make-neighborhood-safer-place/.

- **"How to Use Nextdoor for Crime Prevention."** This article explains how to use the Nextdoor social media app to help prevent crime in your neighborhood by keeping in touch with your neighbors. https://help.nextdoor.com/s/article/About-Nextdoor-for-crime-prevention?language=en_US.

- **National Neighborhood Watch.** This website can help you search for a neighborhood watch program in your area or register your neighborhood watch group. They also offer training resources and tips on neighborhood safety. www.nnw.org/.

  - **"Starting a Neighborhood Watch."** A handy step-by-step guide to setting up a neighborhood watch program in your community. www.ncpc.org/resources/files/pdf/neighborhood-safety/nwstart.pdf.

- **Neighborhood Safety Network.** From the Consumer Product Safety Commission, this resource offers tools to keep you safe in your home and in the area surrounding it. www.cpsc.gov/en/Safety-Education/Neighborhood-Safety-Network/.

- **"Taking Back Your Neighborhood."** This guide from the NCPC explains how you can reclaim your neighborhood by coordinating closely with neighbors and local police. https://www.ncpc.org/wp-content/uploads/2017/11/takeback.pdf.

- **Tools and Resources to Help You Start or Maintain a Neighborhood Watch Program.** From the NCPC, this Neighborhood Watch resource will help you set up a new program in your community or maintain your current Neighborhood Watch Program. https://www.ncpc.org/resources/home-neighborhood-safety/neighborhood-watch/.

- **"What Do You Say When...?"** The City of Minneapolis Police Department offers answers for some of the objections you may get to setting up a neighborhood watch program.

Neighborhood Safety Checklists

Checklists and surveys are a quick and easy way to keep organized and ensure your neighborhood's safety by preventing crime. Here are a few you may find useful.

- **"Home Security Checklist."** This checklist from the NCPC can help you identify security risks at home and threats to safety in your neighborhood. https://www.ncpc.org/wp-content/uploads/2017/11/homechk2.pdf

- **"Neighborhood Checkup Survey."** Your neighbors can fill out this survey from the NCPC to help you identify safety hazards and security issues in your community. https://www.ncpc.org/wp-content/uploads/2017/11/neighborhood-safety-survey.pdf.

How Technology Can Help

There are some useful apps that can help you stay in touch with neighbors and people in elected positions in your community. Here are some suggested ways to connect without leaving your home.

- Form a Facebook group.

- Check out Nextdoor.

- Teach kids (your own and those in the neighborhood) about social media safety.

- Use these services to receive updates on criminals and other dangers in your community.

    - **CrimeMapping.com** offers up-to-date information on criminals and sex offenders in your community.

    - **CrimeReports** will provide you with information on crimes that have happened in your area. www.crimereports.com/.

    - **Family Watchdog** is a free service that will show you where registered sex offenders and other criminals live. You can sign up for free updates to get alerted when one moves in or out of your community. www.familywatchdog.us/.

    - **Neighborhood Scout** can help provide you key information on crime, sex offenders, and more. www.neighborhoodscout.com/.

    - **SpotCrime** can help you learn about criminal activities such as arson, assaults, burglaries, robberies, theft, and vandalism in your neighborhood. www.spotcrime.com/.

AFTERWORD

I have followed Marita Golden's career from afar, but with great interest, for quite some time. As the author of seventeen books and counting, she has enough experience and exposure to garner attention from anyone with ambitions to emulate her. Marita Golden is a novelist, a nonfiction author, an educator and activist, and the co-founder of the Hurston/Wright Foundation. She has led students in classrooms across the United States, including Emerson College and George Mason University, as well as internationally in Lagos, Nigeria. Her books have the unique ability to grip readers and take them on unforgettable journeys of discovery, through the lens of African-American characters who are either grappling with history or experiencing the intricacies of love or political commitment. And so it is no surprise that this book, *Saving Our Sons*, awakens something in me.

Saving Our Sons **is one of the most important pieces of literature for Black parents**, especially Black mothers raising sons in America. Like Golden, I am an educator. As such, I find myself connected to young people daily. I was already learning the importance of communication between those students and myself, and reading this book pushed me out of my comfort zone and into the tumultuous and love-filled struggle that is parenthood. I am stunned at what this book promises to accomplish and in how graciously it delivers, without presumption but with experience, on the truth about raising Black sons in this country.

What I find interesting is that Golden herself, although born in the '50s, does not again assume a place of arrogance for knowing more than the rest of us. She has lived through an America that seems eager to shake off and detach itself from the darkness of racism and injustice. There is no judgment anywhere here; what I do find is love and dedication. It fills the heart of a reader with desire to keep reading, to learn more. What is it like to be a Black mother in America? What would she not give to see her son through this world, to ensure he makes it out alive? What struck me was how relevant these questions still are today, how much they still matter. What has changed? Not much, sadly. First published in 1995, little has changed in terms of prospects for Black boys, who are more prone to violence and imprisonment than any other group of young people today. Fully cognizant of these facts and filled with trepidation, Golden's journey as a mother as written in these pages is also a call to action for society to step in and adopt our youth as our own, creating a village to raise children who too often fall short of their potential, die violent deaths, become sick, or lose their meager freedom in the school-to-prison pipeline.

Marita Golden's *Saving Our Sons* is a roadmap to raising a Black son, and a cautionary tale. Golden writes of the challenges of bringing her son Michael, a young Black child, to adulthood with a clear-eyed authority that comes from her own experience and from a journalistic understanding of the statistics and stories related to Black youths. We are now in 2022. We're still not riding around in flying cars, and so much of everything else is the same. Around the country, every day of every year is the last day for a young Black man, lost to the devastating blow of gun violence. The stories populate our airwaves and our television sets, and our cell phones report incidents and altercations between a Black man and a policeman, or a Black man caught in the line of fire. How do we save these young men from the grips of hate? How do we save them from themselves? How do we teach these children when they're young and raise them to be upstanding men who can show up for their communities, men upon whom their communities can rely? When they are men, how do we pledge allegiance to them, believe in them, and build them up when the entire world is constantly tearing them down? How do we remind them that they are strong and capable, and bold? How can we ensure that they respect their bodies and those of others, that they will respect and protect women?

In *Saving our Sons*, Marita Golden shares her experience as a mother raising her son while single, disconnecting her child from his paternal roots in order to protect him. Even women who have not mothered children will empathize. This book is a toolbox filled with Golden's talent. Her way with words paints a vivid picture of Black motherhood, to show us readers where the struggle is and how she stirred the ship to port even when the path was uncertain. In addition to setting the stage for her son Michael and his set of challenges, Golden weaves in the stories of students who have impacted her life and taught her valuable lessons on change and how profound it can be. Along with her own story, Golden examines the stories of young men like Len and Jay Bias, and Terrance Brown, who had sparkling possible futures and somehow lost their way or were prematurely taken from us for no logical reason. She treats these stories with the care and respect they deserve, and in the process shows exactly how terrifying it can be to mother a Black son, and how easily it can all go awry.

Through her own experience, Golden also shows that it is possible to raise a Black son to be a strong and courageous adult, and to defy the statistics through diligence, communication, and love. If anything is apparent in the pages of this book, it is how powerful a force love can be in parenting. Love by itself is not enough always, but it is the surest bet our young men have in forging a successful journey into adulthood.

This book is a remarkable ode to Black men—to those who, present in Golden's life, have impacted her and her son in some way. The father figures who were neighbors, relatives, uncles, sometimes even her lovers. As an educator, I have seen scores of students enter and leave my classrooms shouldering the burden of their fathers' absences, and it reflects on gaps in our communities that too often affect our children. *Saving Our Sons* is a guidebook for those of us who want to build stronger, mindful men who are proud leaders and fierce thinkers. I admire Marita Golden's journey into establishing connections for her son: giving him a sense of belonging; retying him even to his father from whom she had distanced herself; taking him back to Nigeria where, in his young adulthood, he could meet his grandmother and uncle, and other relatives.

The relationship between a Black mother and her son is a sacred trust. I am continually reminded that, as he was dying, George Floyd called out not to God but to his mama. Black mothers are more likely to raise their children in single parent homes, without the added support of a father to help raise them. Yet, Golden encourages mothers to forgive the shortcomings of the fathers of Black boys and, where possible, to forge bonds with their absent fathers. Her own son's journey to reunite with his father in Lagos, Nigeria, helped shape Michael's future and led to a reconciliation that no doubt strengthened the bond between mother and son.

Golden's book is as relevant now as when it was first written, maybe even more so. In her epilogue, she produces a partial list of the names of fallen sons who were killed in the Washington, DC, area between 1988 and when her book was first published. How exponentially longer that list would be today if it were updated. *Saving Our Sons* is a book about hope and dreams for the future, and as long as Black boys are dying unnatural deaths, it should be read and re-read, again and again, until it's no longer necessary and pertinent.

-MJ FIEVRE
Educator, author of *Raising Confident Black Kids*

ACKNOWLEDGEMENTS

Thanks to Clyde McElvene, to Patricia Elam Ruff, to my husband, Joe Murray, and to my agent, Carol Mann, who read early drafts of this manuscript and provided enormously helpful conversations and dialogues. I thank as well Ella Ross, Terrance Brown, Joyce Ladner, Marc Richardson, James and Lonise Bias, and others for allowing me to invade their lives, secrets, and thoughts. I thank them for the trust they gave, which I sought diligently not to abuse as I told their story and mine.

ABOUT THE AUTHOR

Marita Golden is a veteran teacher of writing and an acclaimed award-winning author of seventeen works of fiction, nonfiction, and anthologies. As a teacher of writing, she has served as a member of the faculties of the MFA Graduate Creative Writing Programs at George Mason University and Virginia Commonwealth University and in the MA Creative Writing Program at Johns Hopkins University, as well as at the University of the District of Columbia and the University of Lagos in Nigeria. As a literary consultant, she offers writing workshops, coaching, and manuscript evaluation services.

Books by Marita Golden include: the novels *The Strong Black Woman: How a Myth Endangers the Physical and Mental Health of Black Women*, *The Wide Circumference of Love*, *After*, and *The Edge of Heaven*; the memoirs *Migrations of the Heart* and *Don't Play in the Sun: One Woman's Journey Through the Color Complex*; and the anthology *Us Against Alzheimer's: Stories of Family Love and Faith*. She is the recipient of many awards, including the Writers for Writers Award presented by Barnes & Noble and Poets and Writers, an award from the Authors Guild, and the Fiction Award for her novel *After* from the Black Caucus of the American Library Association.

As a literary activist, Marita cofounded and serves as President Emerita of the Zora Neale Hurston/ Richard Wright Foundation.

Mango Publishing, established in 2014, publishes an eclectic list of books by diverse authors—both new and established voices—on topics ranging from business, personal growth, women's empowerment, LGBTQ studies, health, and spirituality to history, popular culture, time management, decluttering, lifestyle, mental wellness, aging, and sustainable living. We were recently named 2019 *and* 2020's #1 fastest-growing independent publisher by *Publishers Weekly*. Our success is driven by our main goal, which is to publish high-quality books that will entertain readers as well as make a positive difference in their lives.

Our readers are our most important resource; we value your input, suggestions, and ideas. We'd love to hear from you—after all, we are publishing books for you!

Please stay in touch with us and follow us at:

> Facebook: Mango Publishing
> Twitter: @MangoPublishing
> Instagram: @MangoPublishing
> LinkedIn: Mango Publishing
> Pinterest: Mango Publishing
> Newsletter: mangopublishinggroup.com/newsletter

Join us on Mango's journey to reinvent publishing, one book at a time.

FEB 0 3 2023

CPSIA information can be obtained
at www.ICGtesting.com
Printed in the USA
JSHW032036090522
25756JS00003B/105